W9-CDV-379

A Dictionary of
Sexist Quotations

A
Dictionary of
Sexist
Quotations

Simon James
Lecturer in Economics
University of Exeter

THE HARVESTER PRESS · SUSSEX
BARNES & NOBLE BOOKS · NEW JERSEY

First published in Great Britain in 1984 by
THE HARVESTER PRESS LIMITED
Publisher: John Spiers
16 Ship Street, Brighton, Sussex

and in the USA by
BARNES & NOBLE BOOKS
81 Adams Drive, Totowa, New Jersey 07512

British Library Cataloguing in Publication Data
James, Simon, 1952—
    A dictionary of Sexist quotations.
    1. Men–Quotations, maxims, etc.
    2. Women–Quotations, maxims, etc.
    I. Title
    305.3   PN6084.M4

    ISBN 0-7108-0483-0

Library of Congress Cataloging in Publication Data
Main entry under title:
A Dictionary of sexist quotations.
    1. Sex role–Dictionaries.   2. Sex role–Anecdotes,
facetiae, satire, etc. 3. Sexism–Dictionaries.
4. Sexism–Anecdotes, facetiae, satire, etc. I. James,
Simon R.
HQ1075.D52 1984   305.3'03'21   84-11108
ISBN 0-389-20501-X

Typeset in 11/12 point Bembo by Preface Ltd, Salisbury, Wilts.
Printed in Great Britain by Whitstable Litho Ltd, Whitstable, Kent

Neither side will win the sex
war as there is far too much
fraternization with the enemy.

Anonymous.

Contents

List of Topics

Preface

In his book *Our Women, Chapters on the Sex-Discord*, Arnold Bennett wrote 'Who wants the sex-discord to be resolved? The sex-discord may be the most exasperating thing in existence, but it is by general agreement the most delightful and the most interesting.' While some people certainly find it extremely exasperating, there seems to be little sign that the sex-discord will ever be resolved. Indeed, the ancient rivalry between the sexes continues to produce an enormous number of interesting comments and observations.

The quotations that follow are arranged by topic and a list of these appears on page ix. The allocation of quotations between topics is sometimes rather arbitrary because, of course, many quotations refer to two or more subjects. However, the key-word index should enable the reader to find particular quotations without too much difficulty.

The key-word index gives a two-figure reference for each quotation in which the key word has an important part. The first figure refers to the number of the topic and the second to the quotation itself. Part of the quotation is also given to indicate the context. For example, the entry under 'accident' reads: 'The male is an a. 40.2'. This refers to the second quotation appearing under the 40th topic, which is 'The Female'. The full quotation is then 'The male is an accident: the female would have sufficed.' The numbers and titles of the topics appear at the tops of the pages, and within each topic the quotations are arranged alphabetically by author or source.

There is also an index of authors and sources on page 159.

While the dates of birth and death have been given wherever possible for deceased authors, no attempt has been made to provide the dates of birth of living persons.

The original idea for this book was supplied by Edward Elgar of The Harvester Press. I hope he likes the result. Thanks are also due to Jane Black, Peter Dolton, Krystyna Grycuk, Alan James, R. H. Parker and Chantal Stebbings for valuable suggestions. I should also like to express my gratitude for the generous and patient help given by the staff of a number of libraries. Finally, if anyone is offended by the sexist nature of the contents, it serves them right!

Simon James

Exeter
January 1984

Quotations

1. Adam and Eve

1. You see, dear, it is not true that woman was made from man's rib; she was really made from his funny bone.
    > J. M. Barrie (1860–1937) *What Every Woman Knows*, 1908.

2. I wish Adam had died with all his ribs in his body.
    > Dion Boucicault (1822–1890). Quoted in N. Bentley and E. Esar, *The Treasury of Humorous Quotations*.

3. And Adam, sure, could with more ease abide
    The bone when broken, than when made a bride.
    > William Congreve (1670–1729) *The Old Bachelor*, 1693, V. v.

4. For women, with a mischief to their kind,
    Pervert with bad advice, our better mind,
    A woman's counsel brought us first to woe,
    And made her man his paradise forgo.
    > John Dryden (1631–1700) *The Cock and the Fox*, 1700, l.555.

5. When Eve upon the first of men
    The apple pressed with specious cant,
    Oh! what a thousand pities then
    That Adam was not adamant.
    > Thomas Hood (1799–1845) *A Reflection*.

6. Man created woman—out of what? Out of a rib of his god—of his ideal.

    > Friedrich Nietzsche (1844–1900) *The Twilight of the Idols*, 1888, 'Maxims and Missiles', 13.

7. Whatever you say against women, they are better creatures than men; for men were made of clay, but woman was made of man.

    > Jonathan Swift (1667–1745) *Polite Conversation*, 1738, I.

8. I sometimes think that if Adam and Eve had been merely engaged, she would not have talked with the serpent; and the world would have been saved an infinity of misery.

    > H. G. Wells (1866–1946) *Select Conversations with an Uncle*, 1895.

9. Think how poor Mother Eve was brought
    To being as God's afterthought.

    > Anna Wickham (1884–1947) *To Men*.

2. Adultery

(Cuckold—The husband of an adulteress)

1. Call your husband a cuckold in jest, and he'll never suspect you.

    > H. G. Bohn (1796–1884) *Handbook of Proverbs*, 1855.

2. Reading someone else's newspaper is like sleeping with someone else's wife. Nothing seems to be precisely in the right place, and when you find what you are looking for, it is not clear then how to respond to it.

    > Malcolm Bradbury, *Stepping Westward*, 1965, book I, ch. 1.

3. What men call gallantry, and gods adultery,
    Is much more common where the climate's sultry.
    > Lord Byron (1788–1824) *Don Juan*,
    > canto I, 1819, st. lxiii.

4. But yet is merely innocent flirtation,
    Not quite adultery, but adulteration.
    > Lord Byron (1788–1824) *ibid.* canto XII,
    > 1823, st. lxiii.

5. Husbands cannot be *principals* in their own cuckoldom,
    but they are *parties* to it much more often than they
    themselves imagine.
    > C. C. Colton (1780–1832) *Lacon*, 1820, vol. I, 377.

6. If the spirit of cuckoldom be once raised up in a woman,
    the devil can't lay it, 'till she had done't.
    > William Congreve (1670–1729) *The Old Bachelor*,
    > 1693, I. i.

7. I say I don't sleep with married men, but what I mean is
    that I don't sleep with happily married men.
    > Britt Ekland, *Observer*, 'Sayings of the Week',
    > 16 September 1979.

8. Better to be a cuckold and no one know it, than to be
    none and yet to be thought so.
    > James Howell (*c.* 1594–1666) *Proverbs*, 1659.

9. Confusion of progeny constitutes the essence of the
    crime; and therefore a woman who breaks her marriage
    vows is much more criminal than a man who does it.
    > Samuel Johnson (1709–1784) *Boswell's Life*,
    > Spring 1768.

10. *Boswell*: To be sure there is a great difference between
    the offence of infidelity in a man and that of his wife.
    Johnson: The difference is boundless. The man imposes
    no bastards upon his wife.
    > Samuel Johnson (1709–1784) *Boswell's Life*,
    > 10 October 1779.

3. Advertising

1. Women come in two types: young and not so young.

    Anonymous; advertising maxim.

2. Doing business without advertising is like winking at a girl in the dark. You know what you are doing, but nobody else does.

    Steuart Henderson Britt. Attributed.

3. Advertising is an incredibly powerful agent of male supremacy.

    Jill Nicholls and Pat Moan, *Spare Rib*, 72, July 1978.

4. Advice

1. A woman seldom asks advice before she has bought her wedding clothes.

    Joseph Addison (1672–1719) *The Spectator*, no. 475, 4 September 1712.

2. Never sleep with a woman whose troubles are worse than your own.

    Nelson Algren. Quoted in L. J. Peter, *Peter's Quotations*.

3. How hard it is for women to keep counsel.

    William Shakespeare (1564–1616) *Julius Caesar*, 1599–1600, II. iv.

5. Age

1. Young men soon give, and soon forget affronts;
   Old age is slow in both—A false old traitor!

    Joseph Addison (1672–1719) *Cato*, 1721, II. v.

4

2. All old men do foolish things
    When they marry young wives.
    > Anonymous, *The Female Wits, c.* 1697, act III.

3. A man is as old as he feels, and a woman as old as she looks.
    > Anonymous.

4. Men are worried about how many years they have left, women how many they have had.
    > Anonymous.

5. Men of age object too much, consult too long, adventure too little, repent too soon, and seldom drive business home to the full period, but content themselves with a mediocrity of success.
    > Francis Bacon (1561–1626) *Essays*, 1597, XLII,
    > 'Of Youth and Age'.

6. Ladies even of the most uneasy virtue
    Prefer a spouse whose age is short of thirty.
    > Lord Byron (1788–1824) *Don Juan*,
    > canto I, 1819, st. lxii.

7. A lady of a 'certain age', which means
    Certainly agéd.
    > Lord Byron (1788–1824) *ibid.* canto VI, 1823, st. lxix.

8. Some reckon women by their suns or years,
    I rather think the moon should date the dears.
    > Lord Byron (1788–1824) *ibid.* canto X, 1823, st. x.

9. An archaeologist is the best husband any woman can have: the older she gets the more he is interested in her.
    > Agatha Christie (1891–1975) *Observer*, 'Sayings of the
    > Week', 2 January 1955.

10. A man is as old as he's feeling,
    A woman as old as she looks.
    > Mortimer Collins (1827–1876) *The Unknown
    > Quantity*.

11.   They say women and music should never be dated.

Oliver Goldsmith (1728–1774) *She Stoops to Conquer*, 1775, act III.

12.   I have heard it said that one should be a girl, and a good–looking girl, between thirteen and twenty-two, and after that become a man.

Jean de La Bruyère (1645–1696) *Characters*, 1688, 'Of Women', 3.

13.   My mother used to say it was a great relief to her being an old woman because men left her alone.

Jill Nicholls, *Spare Rib*, 72, July 1978.

14.   The man who is younger than he ought to be is always no better than he should be.

Arthur Wing Pinero (1855–1934) *The Gay Lord Quex*, 1899, act II.

15.   No man under forty-five is worth wasting a minute's time over.

Arthur Wing Pinero (1855–1934) *ibid*

16.   The years a woman subtracts from her age are not lost. They are added to other women's.

Diane de Poitiers (1499–1566). Quoted in W. H. Auden and L. Kronenberger, *The Faber Book of Aphorisms*.

17.   When men reach their sixties and retire, they go to pieces. Women just go right on cooking.

Gail Sheehy. Quoted in B. Rowe, *The Book of Quotes*.

18.   I swear she's no chicken, she's on the wrong side of thirty, if she be a day.

Jonathan Swift (1667–1745) *Polite Conversation*, 1738, I.

19. If a man would register all his opinions upon love, politics, religion, learning, and the like; beginning from his youth, and so go on to old age: what a bundle of inconsistencies and contradictions would appear at last?

> Jonathan Swift (1667–1745) *Thoughts on Various Subjects*, 1711.

20. Dignity and station, or great riches, are in some sort necessary to old men, in order to keep the younger at a distance, who are otherwise too apt to insult them upon the score of their age.

> Jonathan Swift (1667–1745) *ibid.*

21. Every man desires to live long: but no man would be old.

> Jonathan Swift (1667–1745) *ibid.*

22. Men become old, but they never become good.

> Oscar Wilde (1854–1900) *Lady Windermere's Fan*, 1892, act I.

23. One should never trust a woman who tells one her real age. A woman who would tell one that, would tell one anything.

> Oscar Wilde (1854–1900) *A Woman of No Importance*, 1893, act I.

6. Anger

1. I should rail at you, but you are a woman,
    And anger's lost upon you.

> Francis Beaumont (1584–1616) and John Fletcher (1579–1625) *The Scornful Lady*, 1616, III. i.

2. He shall find no fiend in hell can match the fury of a disappointed woman!—Scorned! slighted! dismissed without a parting pang.

> Colley Cibber (1671–1757) *Love's Last Shift*, 1696, IV. i.

7

3. Heav'n has no rage, like love to hatred turn'd,
   Nor Hell a fury, like a woman scorn'd.
   William Congreve (1670–1729) *The Mourning Bride*,
   1697, III. viii.

4. But men are men; the best sometimes forget:—
   Though Cassio did some little wrong to him,—
   As men in rage strike those that wish them best.
   William Shakespeare (1564–1616) *Othello*,
   1604–5, II. iii.

7. Argument

1. Arguments out of a pretty mouth are unanswerable.
   Joseph Addison (1672–1719) *Women and Liberty*, in
   J. R. Green, *Essays of Joseph Addison*.

2. With women the heart argues, not the mind.
   Matthew Arnold (1822–1888) *Merope*, 1858, p. 21.

3. Men are so made that they can resist sound argument,
   and yet yield to a glance.
   Honoré de Balzac (1799–1850) Attributed.

4. A quarrel may end wi' the whip, but it begins wi' the
   tongue, and it's the women have got the most o' that.
   George Eliot (1819–1880) *Daniel Deronda*, 1876,
   book IV, ch 31.

5. The bed with a wife in it is always full of quarrels and
   bickering: there is never any sleep to be had there.
   Juvenal (*c.* AD 60–*c.* 140) *Satires*, VI.

6. Women must have the last word.
   Proverb, 16th century.

7. Like her sex in general, she had disputed his little point,
   merely for the sake of disputing it.
   Johann Paul Friedrich Richter (1763–1825) *Flower,*
   Fruit and Thorn Pieces, 1845, book II, ch. V.

8. A woman finds it much easier to yield and say nothing when she is in the right than when she is in the wrong.
    Johann Paul Friedrich Richter (1763–1825)
    ibid. ch. VI.

9. It is impossible to persuade a man who does not disagree, but smiles.
    Muriel Spark, *The Prime of Miss Jean Brodie*,
    1962, ch. 3.

10. The book of female logic is blotted all over with tears, and justice in their courts is for ever in a passion.
    William Makepeace Thackeray (1811–1863) *The Virginians*, 1857, vol. I, ch. IV.

8. Art

1. A woman has no greater rival than the art of an artist; and the jealousy between one woman and another is mild in comparison with the jealousy which may animate a woman against the art of the artist who has captured her.
    Arnold Bennett (1867–1931) *Our Women*, 1920, ch. 1.

2. Modern art is what happens when painters stop looking at girls and persuade themselves they have a better idea.
    John Ciardi. Quoted in L. J. Peter, *Peter's Quotations*.

3. The female nude—passive, available, devoid of individual desires, her body a blank canvas for man's creativity—is a major subject of art in our culture.
    Rozsika Parker, *Spare Rib*, 54, January 1977.

4. Of all human struggles there is none so treacherous and remorseless as the struggle between the artist man and the mother woman.
    George Bernard Shaw (1856–1950) *Man and Superman*, 1903, act I.

9. Aunts

1. As cold as an aunt's kiss.

Anonymous.

2. If my aunt had wheels, she would be a bus.

Proverb.

3. Susan Mebberley was a charming woman, but she was also an aunt.

Saki (1870–1916) *The Chronicles of Clovis*,
1911, 'Adrian'.

4. Lucas, realizing that Susan Mebberley was a woman as well as an aunt, saw that she would have to be allowed to have her own way.

Saki (1870–1916) *ibid.*

5. Dahlia . . . being my good and deserving aunt, not to be confused with Aunt Agatha, who eats broken bottles and wears barbed wire next to the skin.

P. G. Wodehouse (1881–1975) *The Code of The Woosters*, 1938 ch. I.

6. It is no use telling me that there are bad aunts and good aunts. At the core, they are all alike. Sooner or later, out pops the cloven hoof.

P. G. Wodehouse (1881–1975) *ibid.* ch. 2.

10. Bachelors

1. A bachelor's life is one undarned thing after another.

Anonymous.

2. A bachelor is a man who enjoys the hunt but not the kill.

Anonymous.

3.   While you're single your pockets jingle.

Anonymous.

4.   It is a truth universally acknowledged, that a single man in possession of a good fortune must be in need of a wife.

Jane Austen (1775–1817) *Pride and Prejudice*, 1813, ch 1.

5.   Unmarried men are best friends, best masters, best servants; but not always best subjects; for they are light to run away; and almost all fugitives are of that condition.

Francis Bacon (1561–1626) *Essays*, 1597, VIII, 'Of Marriage and Single Life'.

6.   Certainly wife and children are a kind of discipline of humanity; and single men, though they may be many times more charitable, because their means are less exhaust, yet, on the other side, they are more cruel and hard-hearted (good to make severe inquisitors), because their tenderness is not so often called upon.

Francis Bacon (1561–1626) *ibid.*

7.   The attitude towards marriage of the heart-free bachelor must be at best a highly cautious attitude. He knows he is already in the frying-pan (none knows better), but, considering the propinquity of the fire, he doubts whether he had not better stay where he is. His life will be calmer, more like that of a hibernating snake; his sensibilities will be dulled; but the chances of poignant suffering will be very much reduced.

Arnold Bennett (1867–1931) *Mental Efficiency*, 1911, 'Marriage'.

8.   A lewd bachelor makes a jealous husband.

H. G. Bohn (1796–1884) *A Handbook of Proverbs*, 1855.

11

9. That's what a man wants in a wife, mostly; he wants to make sure o' one fool as 'ull tell him he's wise. But there's some men can do wi'out that—they think so much o' themselves a'ready; an' that's how it is there's old bachelors.

    George Eliot (1819–1880) *Adam Bede*, 1859, ch. 53.

10. We bachelors laugh and show our teeth, but you married men laugh till your hearts ache.

    George Herbert (1593–1633) *Jacula Prudentum*, 1651.

11. A man without a wife is only half a man.

    Sanskrit proverb.

12. Give women the vote, and in five years there will be a crushing tax on bachelors.

    George Bernard Shaw (1856–1950) *Man and Superman*, 1903, Epistle Dedicatory.

13. When an old bachelor marries a young wife—he deserves—no the crime carries the punishment along with it.

    Richard Brinsley Sheridan (1751–1816) *The School for Scandal*, 1777, I. ii.

14. Bachelor's fare, bread and cheese, and kisses.

    Jonathan Swift (1667–1745) *Polite Conversation*, 1738, I.

15. Damme, sir, it is your duty to get married. You can't be always living for pleasure.

    Oscar Wilde (1854–1900) *An Ideal Husband*, 1899, act III.

16. It's perfectly scandalous the amount of bachelors who are going about society. There should be a law passed to compel them to marry within twelve months.

    Oscar Wilde (1854–1900) *A Woman of No Importance*, 1893, act II.

11. Beauty

1. Most girls prefer beauty to brains because they know men can see a lot better than they can think.

   Anonymous.

2. Stop Miss World—we want to get off.

   Anonymous—banner at a demonstration against the Miss World beauty competition.

3. Beauty, *n*. The power by which a woman charms a lover and terrifies a husband.

   Ambrose Bierce (1842–*c*.1914) *The Devil's Dictionary*, 1911.

4. A beautiful woman is paradise for the eyes, hell for the soul, and purgatory for the purse.

   Nicolas Chamfort (1741–1794) Attributed

5. Women have in general but one object, which is their beauty; upon which scarce any flattery is too gross for them to follow.

   Lord Chesterfield (1694–1773) Letter to his son, 16 October 1747.

6. Beauty is a talisman which works true miracles, and, without a fable, transforms mankind.

   Hannah Cowley (1743–1809) *Who's the Dupe?* 1779, act II.

7. Women are everywhere conscious of the value of their own beauty; and when they have the means, they take more delight in decorating themselves with all sorts of ornaments than do men.

   Charles Darwin (1809–1892) *The Descent of Man*, 1871, part III, ch. XX.

8. Tell a woman she's a beauty and the Devil will tell her so ten times.

   Thomas Fuller (1654–1734) *Gnomologia*, 1732.

9. She has beauty enough to make any woman alive hate her.

> John Gay (1685–1732) *Polly*, 1729, act I.

10. He that weds a beauty
    Soon will find her cloy;
    When pleasure grows a duty
    Farewell love and joy:
    He that weds for treasure
    (Though he hath a wife)
    Hath chose one lasting pleasure
    In a married life.

> John Gay (1685–1732) *ibid.*, Air II.

11. Plain women know more about men than beautiful ones do.

> Katherine Hepburn. Quoted in C. Higham, *Kate*.

12. There are few women whose worth lasts longer than their beauty.

> François, Duc de La Rochefoucauld (1613–1680)
> *Maxins*, 1678.

13. Not ten yoke of oxen
    Have the power to draw us
    Like a woman's hair!

> Henry Wadsworth Longfellow (1807–1882) *Tales of a Wayside Inn*, 1864, 'The Saga of King Olaf'. XVI.

14. Gentlemen always seem to prefer blondes.

> Anita Loos (1893–1981) *Gentlemen Prefer Blondes*, 1925, ch. 1.

15. Good looks are almost a stigma. You have to try harder to prove you're intelligent.

> Debra Sue Maffet—retiring Miss America *Observer*, 'Sayings of the Week', 25 September 1983.

16. A woman may be as wicked as she likes, but if she isn't pretty it won't do her much good.

> W. Somerset Maugham (1874–1966) *A Writer's Notebook*, 1896.

17. Any woman you name will pass
As a beauty at night. You should judge jewels or fine cloth
A face or a figure, by day.

> Ovid (43 BC–AD 17) *The Art of Love*, book I.

18. If to her share some female errors fall,
Look on her face, and you'll forget 'em all.

> Alexander Pope (1688–1744) *The Rape of the Lock*, 1712, canto II, l.17.

19. Men have no sense now but for the worthless flower of beauty!

> Richard Brinsley Sheridan (1751–1816) *The Rivals*, 1775, III. iii.

20. Really beautiful women are quite as rare as really intelligent ones.

> C. P. Snow (1905–1980) *The Search*, 1934, ch. 6, 4.

21. Every woman who has beauty may set a price upon herself, and that by underselling the market they ruin the trade.

> Sir John Vanbrugh (1664–1726) *The Relapse*, 1697, IV. ii.

22. It is possible that blondes also prefer gentlemen.

> Momie Van Doren. Attributed.

23. There is nothing sane about the worship of beauty.

> Oscar Wilde (1854–1900) *Intentions*, 1891.

12. Bigamy

(*See also* Polygamy)

1. Bigamy is having one husband too many. Monogamy is the same.

    Anonymous. Quoted in Erica Jong, *Fear of Flying*.

2. Marriage is bound to be a failure if a woman can only have one husband at a time.

    Anonymous.

3. Bigamy, *n*. A mistake in taste for which the wisdom of the future will adjudge a punishment called trigamy.

    Ambrose Bierce (1842–*c*.1914) *The Devil's Dictionary*, 1911.

4. One wife is too much for most husbands to hear
    But two at a time there's no mortal can bear.

    John Gay (1685–1732) *The Beggar's Opera*, 1728, III. xi.

13. Boys

1. Boys will be boys.

    Anonymous.

2. The difference between men and boys is the price of their toys.

    Liberace. Attributed.

3. At school boys become gluttons and slovens, and, instead of cultivating domestic affections, very early rush into the libertinism which destroys the constitution before it is formed; hardening the heart as it weakens the understanding.

    Mary Wollstonecraft (1759–1797) *A Vindication of the Rights of Woman*, 1792, ch. XII.

16

14. Brides

1. Lie still and think of England.
    > Anonymous: Victorian advice to a bride on her
    > wedding night.

2. Brides look so pretty on their wedding day. They are
    often not pretty at other times, but they are all pretty on
    their wedding day.
    > J. M. Barrie (1860–1937) *Barbara's Wedding*, 1918.

3. Bride, *n*. A woman with a fine prospect of happiness
    behind her.
    > Ambrose Bierce (1842–*c*.1914) *The Devil's
    > Dictionary*, 1911.

4. When the men meet a bride, they look at her face; the
    women look at her clothes.
    > E. W. Howe (1853–1937) *Country Town
    > Sayings*, 1911.

5. After all, a man had to make some concessions to his
    bride, especially about the wedding, for women set
    such store by sentimental things.
    > Margaret Mitchell (1900–1949) *Gone With the Wind*,
    > 1936, part IV, ch. 36.

6. It has been said that a bride's attitude towards her
    betrothed can be summed up in the three words: Aisle,
    Altar, Hymn.
    > Frank Muir and Denis Norden, *Oh, My Word!*,
    > 'A Jug of Wine'.

7. He took the bride about the neck,
    And kiss'd her lips with such a clamorous smack
    That, at the parting, all the church did echo.
    > William Shakespeare (1564–1616) *The Taming of the
    > Shrew*, 1593–94, III. ii.

8.   Why should a sane healthy woman be covered up in white gauze like the confectionery in a shop window when there are flies about?

> H. G. Wells (1866–1946) *Select Conversations with an Uncle*, 1895.

15. Careers

1.   We have no desire to say anything that might tend to encourage women to embark on accountancy, for although women might make excellent book-keepers, there is much in accountancy proper that is, we think, unsuitable for them.

> English Institute of Chartered Accountants, *The Accountant*, 14 September 1912, p.341.

2.   A woman's career, particularly if it is successful, is often blamed for the break-up of a marriage, but never a man's.

> Eva Figes, *Patriarchal Attitudes*, 1970, ch. 8.

3.   The percentage of women in management has stuck at between one and two per cent for thirty years. Employers plainly do not think women are a good investment.

> Thomas Kempner. Quoted in *The Times*, 10 February 1983.

4.   There is only one political career for which women are perfectly suitable: diplomacy.

> Clare Boothe Luce. *Observer*, 'Sayings of the Week', 18 April 1982.

5.   Men, in their youth, are prepared for professions, and marriage is not considered as the grand feature in their lives; whilst women, on the contrary, have no other scheme to sharpen their faculties.

> Mary Wollstonecraft (1759–1797) *A Vindication of the Rights of Woman*, 1792, ch. IV.

16. Chastity

1. Girls like to be chaste before they are caught.

    Anonymous.

2. It can be an advantage for a woman to have a reputation for chastity. Chastity itself may also be an advantage sometimes.

    Anonymous.

3. Chaste women are often proud and froward, as presuming upon the merit of their chastity.
    [Froward, no longer used colloquially, meant perverse, difficult to deal with, hard to please, ungovernable.]

    Francis Bacon (1561–1626) *Essays*, 1597, VIII, 'Of Marriage and Single Life'.

4. She is chaste whom nobody has asked.

    Ovid (43 BC–AD 17) *Amores*, book I, 8.

5. The woman who has lost her honour can refuse nothing.

    Tacitus (*c*. AD 55–120) *Annals*, book IV, sec. 3.

6. The little respect paid to chastity in the male world is, I am persuaded, the grand source of many of the physical and moral evils that torment mankind, as well as of the vices and follies that degrade and destroy women.

    Mary Wollstonecraft (1759–1797) *A Vindication of the Rights of Woman*, 1792, ch. XII.

17. Children

1. Bearing babes is a woman's fire and inspiration, and as her womb fills, her head empties.

    Anonymous.

2. Maternity is a matter of fact, paternity is a matter of opinion.

> Anonymous. Quoted by Walter Bagehot, *Physics and Politics*.

3. Mothers have more affection for their children than fathers have: for they have more trouble in giving them birth, and more reassurance that they are their own.

> Aristotle (384–322 BC) *The Nicomachean Ethics*, book IX, ch. 7.

4. The noblest works and foundations have proceeded from childless men; which have sought to express the images of their minds, where those of their bodies have failed: so the care of posterity is most in them that have no posterity.

> Francis Bacon (1561–1626) *Essays*, 1597, VII, 'Of Parents and Children'.

5. Oh, my son's my son till he gets a wife,
   But my daughter's my daughter all her life.

> Dinah Maria Mulock Craik (1826–1887) *Young and Old*.

6. When children cease to be altogether desirable, women cease to be altogether necessary.

> John Langdon-Davies (1897–1971). Quoted in V. Woolf, *A Room of One's Own*.

7. Better than man does woman understand children, but man is more childish than woman.

> Friedrich Nietzsche (1844–1900) *Thus Spake Zarathustra*, 1883–1891, XVIII, 'Old and Young Women'.

8. Man is for woman, a means: the end is always the child. But what is woman for man?

> Friedrich Nietzsche (1844–1900) *ibid*.

9. The one point on which all women are in furious secret rebellion against the existing law is the saddling of the right to a child with the obligation to become the servant of a man.

> George Bernard Shaw (1856–1950) *Getting Married*, 1908, Preface.

10. 'We are the species,' said Mrs Miniver, 'men are only incidents . . . Only in man is the male made the most important. And that happens through our maternity; it's our very importance that degrades us. While we were minding the children they stole our rights and liberties. The children made us slaves, and the men took advantage of it'.

> H. G. Wells (1866–1946) *Ann Veronica*, 1909, ch. II.

18. Chivalry

1. Chivalry today means the woman, right or wrong, just as patriotism today means 'my country right or wrong'. In other words, chivalry today is only another name for Sentimental Feminism.

> E. Belfort Bax (1854–1926) *The Fraud of Feminism*, 1913, ch. V.

2. A desire to have all the fun . . . is nine-tenths of the law of chivalry.

> Dorothy L. Sayers (1893–1957) *Gaudy Night*, 1936, ch. 14.

3. Women are systematically degraded by receiving the trivial attentions which men think it manly to pay to the sex, when in fact, they are insultingly supporting their own superiority.

> Mary Wollstonecraft (1759–1797) *A Vindication of the Rights of Woman*, 1792, ch. IV.

19. Clothes

1. No man objects to the inexpensiveness of his wife's clothes, but every man objects to them looking inexpensive.

   Arnold Bennett (1867–1931) *Self and Self-Management*, 1911, 'The Meaning of Frocks'.

2. Only men who are not interested in women are interested in women's clothes; men who like women never notice what they wear.

   Anatole France (1844–1924). Quoted in N. Bentley and E. Esar, *The Treasury of Humorous Quotations*.

3. A man becomes the creature of his uniform.

   Napoleon I (1769–1821) *Maxims*, 1804–5.

4. The Chinese tame fowls by clipping their wings, and women by deforming their feet. A petticoat round the ankles serves equally well.

   George Bernard Shaw (1856–1950) *Maxims for Revolutionists*, 1903.

5. The substantial reason for our tenacious attachment to the skirt is just this: it is expensive and it hampers the wearer at every turn and incapacitates her for all useful exertion. The like is true of the feminine custom of wearing the hair extremely long.

   Thorstein Veblen (1857–1929) *Theory of the Leisure Class*, 1899, ch. 7.

6. Far too much of a girl's time is taken up in dress.

   Mary Wollstonecraft (1759–1797) *Thoughts on the Education of Daughters*, 1787, 'Dress'.

20. Compliments

(*See also* Flattery)

1. We scarcely thought in our own hall to hear
    This barren verbiage, current among men,
    Light coin, the tinsel clink of compliment.
    > Alfred, Lord Tennyson (1809–1892) *The Princess*,
    > 1847, part II.

2. Women are never disarmed by compliments. Men
    always are.
    > Oscar Wilde (1854–1900) *An Ideal Husband*,
    > 1899, act III.

3. I don't see why a man should think he is pleasing a
    woman enormously when he says to her a whole heap
    of things that he doesn't mean.
    > Oscar Wilde (1854–1900) *Lady Windermere's Fan*,
    > 1892, act I.

21. Conceit

1. Conceit is the finest armour a man can wear.
    > Jerome K. Jerome (1859–1927) *Idle Thoughts of an Idle
    > Fellow*, 1889, 'On being Shy'.

2. The truth is, women who are so puffed up with the
    conceit of talents as to neglect the plain duties of life
    will not frequently be found to be women of the best
    abilities.
    > Hannah More (1745–1833) *Strictures on the Modern
    > system of Female Education*, 1799, ch. XIV.

3. Woman's dearest delight is to wound man's
    self-conceit, though man's dearest delight is to gratify
    hers. There is at least one creature lower than man.
    > George Bernard Shaw (1856–1950) *An Unsocial
    > Socialist*, 1884, ch. 7.

22. Constancy

1. The cruellest revenge of a woman is to remain faithful to a man.

    Jacques Bossuet (1627–1704). Quoted in N. Bentley and E. Esar, *The Treasury of Humorous Quotations*.

2. A constant woman hath but one chance to be happy; an inconstant woman, tho' she hath no chance to be very happy, can never be very unhappy.

    John Gay (1685–1732) *Polly*, 1729, act I.

3. If you are completely devoted to one woman only, then bow your neck to the yoke in voluntary servitude.

    Juvenal (*c.* AD 60–*c.* 140) *Satires*, VI.

4. It is harder to be faithful to a mistress when we are made happy than when we are treated badly.

    François, Duc de La Rochefoucauld (1613–1680) *Maxims*, 1678.

5. The fickleness of the women I love is only equalled by the infernal constancy of the women who love me.

    George Bernard Shaw (1856–1950) *The Philanderer*, 1893, act II.

6. O madam, punctuality is a species of constancy very unfashionable in a lady of quality.

    Richard Brinsley Sheridan (1751–1816) *The School for Scandal*, 1777, IV. iii.

23. Contraception

1. A vasectomy means never having to say you're sorry.

    Anonymous.

2. Skullion had little use for contraceptives at the best of times. Unnatural, he called them, and placed them in

24

the lower social category of things along with elastic-sided boots and made-up bow ties. Not the sort of attire for a gentleman.

> Tom Sharpe, *Porterhouse Blue*, 1974, ch. 9.

3.   Vasectomies and condoms are as safe for women as anything based on men's behaviour can be.

> *Spare Rib*, November 1983. 'A to Z of Feminism: Contraception'.

24. Cooking

(See also Food)

1.   Face powder may catch a man, but it's baking powder that keeps him.

> Anonymous.

2.   Women can spin very well; but they cannot make a good book of cookery.

> Samuel Johnson (1709–1784) *Boswell's Life*, 15 April 1778.

3.   Kissing don't last: cookery do.

> George Meredith (1828–1909) *The Ordeal of Richard Feverel*, 1859, ch. 28.

4.   There is no spectacle on earth more appealing than that of a beautiful woman in the act of cooking dinner for someone she loves.

> Thomas Wolfe (1900–1938) *The Web and the Rock*, 1939.

25. Cosmetics

1.   The ancient British women had the figures of monsters painted on their naked bodies, in order (as our

25

historians tell us) to make themselves beautiful in the eyes of their countrymen, and terrible to their enemies.
Joseph Addison (1672–1719) Politics and the Fan, in
J. R. Green, Essays of Joseph Addison.

2. Deuce take the man who first invented perfumes, say I.
Aristophanes (c.448–c.388 BC) Lysistrata, 411 BC.

3. Most women are not as young as they are painted.
Sir Max Beerbohm (1872–1956) A Defence of
Cosmetics, 1922.

4. A woman that paints put up a bill that she is to be let.
Thomas Fuller (1654–1734) Gnomologia, 1732.

5. Men have often been taken in
By artless beauty. So when she's spreading all that
Mess on her face is another good time—do not be shy—
To visit and inspect her. You will find a thousand pots of
   make-up
Colours and grease, that have melted and run
Down into her sweaty cleavage.
Ovid (43 BC–AD 17) Cures for Love, AD 1.

6. There are no ugly women, only lazy ones.
Helena Rubenstein. Attributed.

7. I have heard of your paintings too, well enough; God has given you one face and you make yourselves another.
William Shakespeare (1564–1616) Hamlet,
1599–1600, III.i.

26. Courage

1. I find I have obstinacy enough to pursue whatever I have once resolved; and a true female courage to oppose anything that resists my will, though 'twere reason itself.

      William Congreve (1670–1729) *The Double-Dealer*, 1694, V. iii.

2. The brave deserve the lovely—every woman may be won.

      Charles Godfrey Leland (1824–1903) Attributed.

3. I have known men of valour, cowards to their wives.

      Jonathan Swift (1667–1745) *Thoughts on Various Subjects*, 1711.

4. Men have more courage than we, so they commit more bold, impudent sins. They quarrel, fight, swear, drink, blaspheme, and the like, whereas we, being cowards, only backbite, tell lies, cheat at cards and so on.

      Sir John Vanbrugh (1664–1726) *The Provok'd Wife*, 1698, V. ii.

27. Courtship

1. A man always chases a woman until she catches him.

      Anonymous.

2. If you want to win her hand,
   Let the maiden understand
   That she's not the only pebble on the beach.

      Harry Braisted, *You're Not the Only Pebble on the Beach*, 1896.

3. All naturally fly what does pursue:
   'Tis fit men should be coy, when women woo.

      William Congreve (1670–1729) *The Old Bachelor*, 1693, IV. ii.

4. Courtship to marriage, is as a very witty prologue to a very dull play.

> William Congreve (1670–1729) *ibid.* V. iv.

5. Oh Polly, you might have toyed and kissed.
   By keeping men off, you keep them on.

> John Gay (1685–1732) *The Beggar's Opera*,
> 1728, I. viii.

6. She who trifles with all
   Is less likely to fall
   Than she who but trifles with one.

> John Gay (1685–1732) *The Coquet Mother and*
> *Coquet Daughter.*

7. Nobody works as hard for his money as the man who marries it.

> Frank McKinney Hubbard (1868–1930). Quoted in
> N. Bentley and E. Esar, *The Treasury of Humorous*
> *Quotations.*

8. 'Margaret's a wise girl' smiled Susie. 'She knows that when a man sends flowers it is a sign that he has admired more women than one.'

> W. Somerset Maugham (1874–1966) *The Magician*,
> 1908, ch. 7.

9. The time I've lost in wooing,
   In watching and pursuing
     The light, that lies
     In woman's eyes,
   Has been my heart's undoing.
   Though wisdom oft has sought me,
   I scorned the lore she brought me,
     My only books
     Were woman's looks,
   And folly's all they've taught me.

> Thomas Moore (1779–1852) *The Time I've Lost*
> *in Wooing.*

10. The first point to understand is that every single
Girl can be caught.
> Ovid (43 BC–AD 17) *The Art of Love*, book I.

11. When a young man complains that a young lady has no
heart, it is a pretty certain sign that she has his.
> George D. Prentice (1802–1870). Quoted in
> N. Bentley and E. Esar, *The Treasury of
> Humorous Quotations*.

12. Nothing was more maddening than to be told by a man
that he had *nearly* invited you out.
> John Winton, *HMS Leviathan*, 1967, ch. 11.

13. There are quite as many male coquets as female, and
they are far more pernicious pests to society, as their
sphere of action is larger, and they are less exposed to
the censure of the world.
> Mary Wollstonecraft (1759–1797) *Thoughts on the
> Education of Daughters*, 1787, 'Love'.

14. Does the imagination dwell the most
Upon a woman won or woman lost?
> W. B. Yeats (1865–1939) *The Tower*, 1928.

28. Crying

1. The greatest water power known to man is woman's
tears.
> Anonymous.

2. Trust not a woman when she cries,
For she'll pump water from her eyes,
With a wet finger.
> Thomas Dekker (*c.* 1570–*c.*1641) *The Honest Whore*,
> 1604, part I, V. i.

3. Tears are never far from a woman's eye.
> Ralph Waldo Emerson (1803–1882) *Journal*, 1837.

4.   Women's weapons, water drops.
>>> William Shakespeare (1564–1616) *King Lear*,
>>> 1605–6, II. iv.

5.   Crying is the refuge of plain women but the ruin of pretty ones.
>>> Oscar Wilde (1854–1900) *Lady Windermere's Fan*,
>>> 1892, act I.

29. Curiosity

1.   Curiosity, *n.* An objectionable quality of the female mind. The desire to know whether or not a woman is cursed with curiosity is one of the most active and insatiable passions of the masculine soul.
>>> Ambrose Bierce (1842–*c.*1914) *The Devil's*
>>> *Dictionary,* 1911.

2.   This is but one way of laying the spirit of curiosity, when once raised in a woman, *viz,* by satisfying it.
>>> Henry Fielding (1707–1754) *The Female*
>>> *Husband,* 1746.

3.   The question a woman always does ask—it being the nature of her sex never to be satisfied—'When will you come again?'
>>> George Bernard Shaw (1856–1950) Letter to
>>> Ellen Terry, 8 September 1896.

4.   You know what a woman's curiosity is. Almost as great as a man's.
>>> Oscar Wilde (1854–1900) *An Ideal Husband,*
>>> 1899, act I.

30. Daughters

1.   Our Polly is a sad slut, nor heeds what we have taught her.
     I wonder any man alive will ever rear a daughter!
>>> John Gay (1685–1732) *The Beggar's Opera,*
>>> 1728, I. viii.

2. Marry your daughters betimes, lest they marry themselves.

> George Herbert (1593–1633) *Jacula Prudentum*, 1651.

3. Fathers, from hence trust not your daughters' minds
   By what you see them act.

> William Shakespeare (1564–1616) *Othello*,
> 1604–5, I. i.

31. Deceit

1. To cheat a man is nothing; but the woman must have fine parts indeed who cheats a woman.

> John Gay (1685–1732) *The Beggar's Opera*,
> 1728, II. iv.

2. What signifies a promise to a woman? Does not man in marriage itself promise a hundred things that he never means to perform?

> John Gay (1685–1732) *ibid*. II. viii.

3. A man can deceive a woman by pretending love, provided he is not in love with someone else.

> Jean de La Bruyère (1645–1696) *Characters*, 1688,
> 'Of Women'.

4. Men are often deceivers, girls hardly ever.

> Ovid (43 BC - AD 17) *The Art of Love,* bk III.

5. Sigh no more, ladies, sigh no more;
       Men were deceivers ever;
   One foot in sea and one on shore,
       To one thing constant never.

> William Shakespeare (1564–1616) *Much Ado About
> Nothing*, 1598–99, II. iii.

31

32. Divorce

1. The only solid and lasting peace between a man and his wife is, doubtless, a separation.
    > Lord Chesterfield (1694–1773). Letter to his son,
    > 1 September 1763.

2. Women were quite ridiculous when it came to judging a man's character. No wonder so many of them ended up in the divorce courts.
    > Richard Gordon, *Doctor on the Boil*, 1970, ch. 5.

3. The wages of sin is alimony.
    > Carolyn Wells (1862–1942) Attributed

33. Drink

1. Man, being reasonable, must get drunk;
    The best of life is but intoxication:
    Glory, the Grape, Love, Gold, in these are sunk
    The hopes of all men, and of every nation;
    Without their sap, how branchless were the trunk
    Of life's strange tree, so fruitful on occasion.
    > Lord Byron (1788–1824) *Don Juan*, canto II,
    > 1819, st. clxxix.

2. I don't mind a man so much, but it makes me feel perfectly terrible to see a girl get intoxicated.
    > Dorothy Parker (1893–1967) *Laments for the Living*,
    > 1930, 'The Last Tea'.

3. Lastly (and this is, perhaps the gold rule), no woman should marry a teetotaller, or a man who does not smoke.
    > Robert Louis Stevenson (1850–1894) *Virginibus*
    > *Puerisque*, 1881, I.

4. Drinking with women is an unnatural as scolding with 'em.

> William Wycherley (1640–1716) *The Country Wife*, 1675, III. ii.

34. Economics

1. We are the only animal species in which the female depends on the male for food, the only animal species in which the sex-relation is also an economic relation.

> Charlotte Perkins Gilman (1860–1935) *Women and Economics*, 1898, ch. 1.

2. The male human being is thousands of years in advance of the female in economic status.

> Charlotte Perkins Gilman (1860–1935) *ibid*.

3. Three women make a market.

> George Herbert (1593–1633) *Jacula Prudentum*, 1651.

4. The corset is, in economic theory, substantially a mutilation, undergone for the purpose of lowering the subject's vitality and rendering her permanently and obviously unfit for work.

> Thorstein Veblen (1857–1929) *Theory of the Leisure Class*, 1899, ch. 7.

35. Education

1. If a woman is allowed to teach advanced studies to both sexes, where afterwards will be the pretended superiority of man? I tell you, the time is near when women will become human beings.

> Anonymous—written following the inaugural lecture of Marie Curie as a professor at the Sorbonne, 1906 and quoted in R. Reid, *Marie Curie*, ch. 13.

2. Whatever men may think about the study of man, women do really believe the noblest study for womankind to be women.

> Samuel Butler (1835–1902) *The Way of All Flesh*, 1903, ch. 28.

3. There are no new ideas about female education. There is not, there never has been, even the vestige of a new idea. All the educational reformers did was to ask what was being done to boys and then go and do it to girls.

> G. K. Chesterton (1874–1936) *What's Wrong With the World*, 1910, part IV, ch. 14, 'Folly and Female Education'.

4. A high degree of intellectual refinement in the female, is the surest pledge society can have for the improvement of the male.

> C. C. Colton (1780–1832) *Lacon*, 1820, vol. I, 137.

5. The charms of women were never more powerful—never inspired such achievements, as in those immortal periods, when they could neither read nor write.

> Hannah Cowley (1743–1809) *Who's the Dupe?*, 1779, act I.

6. We now have, both in public and private, an educational system that treats little boys and little girls very much alike. This is not because the educational system has been altered in spirit, but because girls have simply been absorbed into it.

> Hannah Gavron (1936–1965) *The Captive Wife*, 1966, ch. 16.

7. A woman having a man's education is, given equal beauty, less of a seductress than any other of her sex.

> Remy de Gourmont (1858–1915) *The Natural Philosophy of Love*, 1903, ch. 6.

8. Where there is no education, as in savage countries, men
    will have the upper hand of women.

    > Samuel Johnson (1709–1784) *Boswell's
    > Life*, May 1776.

9. Learned ladies are not to my taste.

    > Molière (1622–1673) *The Learned Ladies*, 1672, I. iii.

10. I would never have an educated man for my husband
    husband.

    > Molière (1622–1673) *ibid*. V. iii.

11. Till women shall be more reasonably educated, and till
    the native growth of their mind shall cease to be stinted
    and cramped, we have no juster ground for
    pronouncing that their understanding has already
    reached its highest attainable point, than the Chinese
    would have for affirming that their women have
    attained to the greatest possible perfection in walking,
    while their first care is, during their infancy, to cripple
    their feet.

    > Hannah More (1745–1833) *Strictures on the Modern
    > System of Female Education*, 1799, ch. XIV.

12. The girls must be trained in precisely the same way [as
    boys], and I say this without any reservations about
    whether horse riding or athletics are suitable for males
    but not females.

    > Plato (*c*. 428–348 BC) *Laws*, book VII, sect. 12.

13. Once it is shown that men and women neither are nor
    ought to be constituted alike either in character or in
    temperament, it follows that they ought not to receive
    the same education.

    > Jean-Jacques Rousseau (1712–1778) *Émile*, 1762,
    > book V, part I.

14. Let a girl's education be as serious as a boy's. You bring up your girls as if they were meant for sideboard ornaments, and then complain of their frivolity.

John Ruskin (1819–1900) *Sesame and Lilies,*
1865, Lecture II.

15. It is the object of a liberal education not only to obscure the knowledge of one sex by another, but to magnify the natural differences between the two.

Robert Louis Stevenson (1850–1894) *Virginibus*
Puerisque, 1881, II.

16. Oh! teach the orphan-boy to read
Or teach the orphan-girl to sew.

Alfred, Lord Tennyson (1809–1892) *Lady Clara Vere*
de Vere, 1832.

17. Higher education has eliminated the witty woman.

H. G. Wells (1866–1946) *Select Conversations with*
an Uncle, 1895.

18. If all the faculties of woman's mind are only to be cultivated as they respect her dependence on man; if, when a husband be obtained, she have arrived at her goal, and meanly proud, rests satisfied with such a paltry crown, let her grovel contentedly, scarcely raised by her employment above the animal kingdom.

Mary Wollstonecraft (1759–1797) *A Vindication of the*
Rights of Woman, 1792, ch. II.

36. Emotion

1. Few of the soft sex are very stable.

Lord Byron (1788–1824) *Don Juan,* canto XV,
1824, st. vi.

2. Most men know what they hate, few what they love.

C. C. Colton (1780–1832) *Lacon,* 1820, vol. I, 525.

3. Like other women, I shall run to extremes. If you won't make me love you, I shall hate you.
John Gay (1685–1732) *Polly*, 1729, act II.

4. You can't trust a woman to stick by you in any scheme that involves her emotions and preferences.
O. Henry (1862–1910) *The Gentle Grafter*, 1908, 'The Exact Science of Matrimony'.

5. The same emotions are present in both man and woman, but in different *tempo*; on which account man and woman never cease to misunderstand each other.
Friedrich Nietzsche (1844–1900) *Beyond Good and Evil*, 1885, ch. IV, 85.

6. Where there is neither love nor hatred in the game, woman's play is mediocre
Friedrich Nietzsche (1844–1900) *ibid*. 115.

7. No passion in a woman can be lasting long.
Samuel Pepys (1633–1703) *Diary*, 29 January 1667.

37. Equality

1. Men their rights and nothing more; women their rights and nothing less.
Susan B. Anthony (1820–1906) *The Revolution*, 1868.

2. The doubtful concept of 'equality in inequality', which the one uses to mask his despotism and the other to mask her cowardice, does not stand the test of experience.
Simone de Beauvoir, *The Second Sex*, 1949, part VII, conclusion.

3. A woman who thinks she is intelligent demands equal rights with men. A woman who *is* intelligent does not.
Collette (1873–1954). Quoted in *The Reader's Digest Treasury of Quotations*.

4. It is folly to imagine that there can be anything very bad in the position of woman compared with that of man, at any time: for since every woman is a man's daughter, and every man is a woman's son, every woman is too near to man, was too recently a man, than that possibly any wide disparity can be. As is the man will be the woman; and as is the woman the man.

    Ralph Waldo Emerson (1803–1882) *Journal*, 1843.

5. When women ask for equality, men take them to be demanding domination.

    Elizabeth Janeway, *Man's World, Woman's Place*, 1971, ch. 19.

6. It's no use women claiming more than men though probably in the end they'll get more as they inevitably do whenever women agitate for equality with men in any respect.

    George Bernard Shaw (1856–1950). Quoted in Antonia Raeburn, *Militant Suffragettes*, ch. 1.

7. It cannot be demonstrated that woman is essentially inferior to man because she has always been subjugated.

    Mary Wollstonecraft (1759–1797) *A Vindication of the Rights of Woman*, 1792, ch. II.

38. Family

1. Woman is the salvation or destruction of the family.

    Henri-Frédéric Amiel (1821–1881) *Journal*, 11 December 1872.

2. He that hath wife and children hath given hostages to fortune; for they are impediments to great enterprises, either of virtue or mischief.

    Francis Bacon (1561–1626) *Essays*, 1597, VIII, 'Of Marriage and Single Life'.

3. Why does society make the sacrifice of woman to the family the chief law of its existence?
    > Honoré de Balzac (1799–1850) *The Memoirs of Two Young Brides*, 1842, ch. XX.

4. When a man is clutched by his family, his deeper social instincts and intuitions are all thwarted, he becomes a negative thing.
    > D. H. Lawrence (1885–1930) *Assorted Articles*, 1930.

5. The female sex wholly govern domestic life: and by this means when they think fit, they can sow dissensions between the dearest friends, may make father and son irreconcilable enemies, in spite of all the ties of gratitude on one part, and the duty of protection to be paid on the other.
    > Sir Richard Steele (1672–1729) *The Spectator*, no. 320, 7 March 1712.

6. The family! Home of all social evils, a charitable institution for indolent women, a prison workshop for the slaving breadwinner, and a hell for children.
    > August Strindberg (1849–1912) *The Son of a Servant*, 1886.

39. Fashion

1. There is not so variable a thing in nature as a lady's head-dress. Within my own memory, I have known it rise and fall above thirty degrees.
    > Joseph Addison (1672–1719) *The Spectator*, no. 98, 11 June 1711.

2. Half a dozen well-dressed men would be indistinguishably alike if you decapitated them. It is notorious that men are the slaves of fashion.
    > Arnold Bennett (1867–1931) *Self and Self-Management*, 1911, 'The Meaning of Frocks'.

3.   The perfect woman must be haughty, but not too beautiful . . . she must be a slave to her clothes and her jewels.

> Salvador Dali. Quoted in M. Rogers,
> *Contradictory Quotations.*

40. The Female

1.   The female has been dominant for the main duration of life on earth.

> Charlotte Perkins Gilman (1860–1935) *Women and Economics*, 1898 ch. VII.

2.   The male is an accident: the female would have sufficed.

> Remy de Gourmont (1858–1915) *The Natural Philosophy of Love*, 1903, ch. 7.

3.   The female of the species is more deadly than the male.

> Rudyard Kipling (1865–1936) *The Female of the Species*, 1911.

41. Femininity

1.   Feminity—thank heaven!—is entirely indestructible.
Arnold Bennett (1867–1931) *Self and Self-Management*, 1911, 'The Meaning of Frocks'.

2.   When she stopped conforming to the conventional picture of femininity she finally began to enjoy being a woman.

> Betty Friedan, *The Feminine Mystique*, 1963 ch. 14.

3.   An acquaintance with the rudiments of physiology will teach you more about feminine character than all the philosophy and wise-saws in the world.

> W. Somerset Maugham (1874–1966) *A Writer's Notebook*, 1896.

42. Feminism

(*See also* Sexism)

1. Put quite simply, feminists do not like real women nor, of course, real men either.

    Anonymous.

2. Women who can, do. Those who cannot, become feminists.

    Anonymous.

3. Women's Lib? Put them behind bras.
    Anonymous: Graffiti, 1971. Quoted in R. Reisner and
    L. Wechsler, *Encyclopaedia of Graffiti*.

4. The feminist pendulum will swing too far. Pendulums always do. (That is why clocks go). As I have before indicated, it is already dangerous in certain circles to doubt whether anything that is possible to men is impossible to women.
    Arnold Bennett (1867–1931) *Our Women*,
    1920, ch. IV.

5. Men are stereotyped [by feminists] into the types of suppressed rapist or the gentle soul conditioned by society to a toughness that hides a natural disposition to weep and wash up.
    Ronald Butt, *The Times*, 18 February 1982.

6. Feminist . . . means, I think, one who dislikes the chief feminine characteristics.
    G. K. Chesterton (1874–1936) *What's Wrong with the
    World*, 1910, part III, ch. 12.

7. He put his arm around her and led her to his car.
    'There are times when even a dedicated feminist needs a chauvinist to lean on.'
    Clive Cussler, *Vixen 03*, 1978, ch. 48.

8. Ridicule has pursued the feminist down the corridors of time like some satanic practical joker; it is almost a relief when the hilarity turns to anger.

    Helen Dudar, 'Women's Lib: The War on Sexism', *Newsweek*, 23 March 1970.

9. Feminism is the most unnatural feminine activity.

    Richard Gordon, *The Facts of Life*, 1969, ch. 3.

10. It is very difficult, from the standpoint of natural logic, to sympathise with moderate feminism, one could more easily accept feminism in excess. For if there are in nature numerous examples of feminism, there are very few of an equality of the sexes.

    Remy de Gourmont (1858–1915) *The Natural Philosophy of Love*, 1903, ch. 7.

11. The new woman's will to live through herself, with herself, for herself, reaches its limit when she begins to regard men merely as a means to a child. Woman would scarcely take a more complete revenge for having herself been treated for thousands of years as a means.

    Ellen Key (1849–1926) *Love and Marriage*, 1911.

12. Since 'liberation' the 'jokes' have gained a new element: a man will now preface his anti-woman cliches with the phrase 'I may be a male chauvinist pig, but . . .'

    Suzanne Lowry, *The Guilt Cage*, 1980.

13. The inheritors of the suffragettes . . . were the women who got the education and franchise and sold it for a mess of domesticity. They gained an empire but didn't know how to lose a role.

    Suzanne Lowry, *ibid.*

14. It was rapidly becoming clear to my mind that men regarded women as a servant class in the community,

and that women were going to remain in the servant class until they lifted themselves out of it.

Emmeline Pankhurst (1858–1928) *My Own Story*, 1914.

15. I think it is very hard for highly educated women to realize how politically naive most women are.

Erin Pizzey. Attributed.

16. Scratch most feminists and underneath there is a woman who longs to be a sex object, the difference is that is not *all* she longs to be.

Betty Rollin. Quoted in J. Green, *A Dictionary of Contemporary Qotations*.

17. The more their sex tries to resemble ours, the less influence they will have over us; and then it is that we shall really be their masters.

Jean-Jacques Rousseau (1712–1778) *Émile*, 1762, book V, part I.

18. There is no 'beginning' of feminism in the sense that there is no beginning to defiance in women.

Sheila Rowbotham, *Women, Resistance and Revolution*, 1973, ch. 1.

19. Modern feminists are no longer so anxious as the feminists of thirty years ago to curtail the 'vices' of men; they ask rather that what is permitted to men shall be permitted also to them. Their predecessors sought equality in moral slavery, whereas they seek equality in moral freedom.

Bertrand Russell (1872–1970) *Marriage and Morals*, ch. VII.

20. To me the expression Ms. really means misery.

Phyllis Schlafly. Quoted in B. Rowe, *The Book of Quotes*.

21.   What women's lib. does to a women who catches the disease is to tell her to put her own self-fulfilment over every other goal and that's just not a view compatible with a happy marriage.

> Phyllis Schlafly. Quoted in *The Sunday Times*,
> 17 January 1982.

22.   If most women continue to see themselves chiefly as reproductive females, they will live and work within the limitations of the weaker sex and the better half. If they choose to see themselves chiefly as human beings, they will live and work as human beings for the better whole.

> Andrew Sinclair, *The Better Half: The Emancipation of
> the American Woman*, 1966, ch. 31.

23.   You can't be a feminist and a capitalist.

> Ruth Wallsgrove, *Observer*, 'Sayings of the Week',
> 25 July 1982.

43. Flattery

(*See also* Compliments)

1.   Most men are fond of flatterers.

> Aristotle (384–322 BC) *Nicomachean Ethics*,
> book VIII, ch. 8.

2.   'Wot's the good o' calling a young 'ooman a wenus or a angel, Sammy?'
'Ah! What, indeed?' replied Sam.
'You might jist as well call her a griffin, or a unicorn, or a king's arms at once, which is werry well known to be a collection o'fabulous animals', added Mr Weller.

> Charles Dickens (1812–1870) *Pickwick Papers*,
> 1837, ch. 33.

3. Wives are like children, the more they are flatter'd and humour'd the more perverse they are.

>> John Gay (1685–1732) *Polly*, 1729, act I.

4. Men generally do so love the taste of flattery, their stomach can never be overcharged with it.

>> Lord Halifax (1633–1695) *Miscellaneous Thoughts and Reflections*, 1750.

5. Oh men for flattery and deceit renowned!
Thus when y'are young, ye learn it all like him,
Till as your years increase, that strengthens too,
T'undo poor maids, and make our ruin easy.

>> Thomas Otway (1652–1685) *The Orphan*, 1680, act I.

6. Flatter and praise, commend, extol their graces;
Though ne'er so black, say they have angels' faces.
That man that hath a tongue, I say, is no man,
If with his tongue he cannot win a woman.

>> William Shakespeare (1564–1616) *Two Gentlemen of Verona*, 1594–95, III. i.

7. Love of flattery in most men proceeds from the mean opinion they have of themselves: in women from the contrary.

>> Jonathan Swift (1667–1745) *Thoughts on Various Subjects*, 1711.

44. Food

(*See also* Cooking)

1. That happiness for Man—the hungry sinner!—
Since Eve ate apples, much depends on dinner.

>> Lord Byron (1788–1824) *Don Juan*, canto XIII, 1823, st. xcix.

2. Feed the Brute!

>> George Du Maurier (1834–1896) *Punch*, 1886.

3. The way to a man's heart is through his stomach.

    Fanny Fern (1811–1872) Attributed.

4. Fond wives do by their husbands as barren wives do by their lap-dogs, cram 'em with sweetmeats till they spoil their stomachs.

    Sir John Vanbrugh (1664–1726) *The Relapse*,
    1697, V. ii.

45. Foolishness

1. Women are most fools when they think th'are wisest.

    Francis Beaumont (1584–1616) and John Fletcher
    (1579–1625) *The Scornful Lady*, 1616, IV. i.

2. If a man does a foolish thing once, he'll hear of it all his life.

    Hannah Cowley (1743–1809) *A Bold Stroke for a
    Husband*, 1784, I. i.

3. It takes a thoroughly good woman to do a thoroughly stupid thing.

    Oscar Wilde (1854–1900) *Lady Windermere's Fan*,
    1892, act II.

4. There's nothing like mixing with women to bring out all the foolishness in a man of sense.

    Thornton Wilder (1897–1975) *The Matchmaker*,
    1954, act I.

46. Forgiveness

1. If you tell your wife everything do you think she will forgive you?

    Anonymous.

2. The women pardoned all except her face.

> Lord Byron (1788–1824) *Don Juan*, canto V,
> 1821, st. cxiii

3. Women never forgive failure.

> Anton Chekhov (1860–1904) *The Seagull*,
> 1896, act II.

4. Most females will forgive a liberty, rather than a slight.

> C. C. Colton (1780–1832) *Lacon*, 1820, vol. I, 557.

5. Once a woman has forgiven her man, she must not reheat his sins for breakfast.

> Marlene Dietrich, *Marlene Dietrich's ABC*.

6. Well, Polly, as far as one woman can forgive another, I forgive thee.

> John Gay (1685–1732) *The Beggar's Opera*,
> 1728, I. viii.

7. Women and elephants never forget an injury.

> Saki (1870–1916) *Reginald on Besetting Sins*, 1904.

47. Friendship

1. A man's friendships are, like his will, invalidated by marriage—but they are also no less invalidated by the marriage of his friends.

> Samuel Butler (1835–1902) *The Way of All Flesh*,
> 1903, ch. 75.

2. A woman can become a man's friend only in the following way: first an acquaintance, then a mistress, and only then a friend.

> Anton Chekhov (1860–1904) *Uncle Vanya*,
> 1897, act II.

3.   No friendship is so cordial or so delicious as that of girl for girl; no hatred so intense and immovable as that of woman for woman.

> Walter Savage Landor (1775–1864) *Imaginary Conversations*, 1826–1829, 'Epicurus, Leontion and Ternissa'.

4.   Men of the same profession are seldom friends, yet there is a much greater number of their fellow-creatures with whom they never clash. But women are very differently situated with respect to each other—for they are all rivals.

> Mary Wollstonecraft (1759–1797) *A Vindication of the Rights of Woman*, 1792, ch. XIII. sect. III.

48. Girls

1.   Always be civil to the girls—you never know whom they may marry.

> Anonymous.

2.   I like being a girl and being feminine. I also like boys. I think being able to have a child is wonderful, whereas boys can only help.

> Anonymous. Quoted in Sue Sharpe, *Just Like a Girl*, Ch. VII.

3.   Wendy, one girl is worth more than twenty boys.

> J. M. Barrie (1860–1937) *Peter Pan*, 1904, act I.

4.   One of those little prating girls
Of whom fond parents tell such tedious stories.

> John Dryden (1631–1700) *The Rival Ladies*, 1664, I. i.

5.   To find out a girl's faults, praise her to her friends.

> Benjamin Franklin (1706–1790) Attributed.

6. Three little maids from school are we,
    Pert as a schoolgirl well can be,
    Filled to the brim with girlish glee!
    Sir W. S. Gilbert (1836–1911) *The Mikado*, 1885, act I.

7. Girls like to be played with, and rumpled a little too, sometimes.
    Oliver Goldsmith (1728–1774) *She Stoops to Conquer*,
    1775, act V.

8. I had often wondered why young women should marry, as they have so much more freedom, and so much more attention paid to them while unmarried, than when married.
    Samuel Johnson (1709–1784) *Boswell's Life*,
    25 March 1776.

9. Any girl can be glamorous: all you have to do is stand still and look stupid.
    Hedy Lamarr. Quoted in L. Halliwell, *The Filmgoer's
    Book of Quotes*.

10. Very innocent girls are usually very stupid girls.
    Compton Mackenzie (1883–1972) *Sinister Street*,
    1913, book I, ch. 10.

11. Girls are so much more difficult to manage than boys. And they begin by being so easy. But after eighteen every month brings a new problem. Their clothes, you know. And of course their behaviour.
    Compton Mackenzie (1883–1972) *ibid*.
    book III, ch. 13.

12. I know not what you write to girls, and yet—
    I know the answer that you never get.
    Martial (*c.* AD 40–*c.* 104) *Epigrams*, trans. Pott and
    Wright, book XI, lxiv.

13. Girls, you know are not like boys. At a certain age they can't be quite natural. It's a bad sign if they don't blush, and fib, and affect this and that.

    George Meredith (1828–1909) *The Ordeal of Richard Feverel*, 1859, ch. 38.

14. No respectable girl ever reads love letters addressed to her: such curiosity would show that she secretly enjoyed that nonsense.

    Molière (1622–1673) *The School for Husbands*, 1661, II. iv.

15. When you see what some girls marry, you realise how they must hate to work for a living.

    Helen Rowland (1876–1950) *Reflections of a Bachelor Girl*, 1909.

16. Since maids, in modesty, say *No* to that
    Which they would have the profferer construe *Ay*.

    William Shakespeare (1564–1616) *Two Gentlemen of Verona*, 1594–95, I. ii.

17. Like all young men, you greatly exaggerate the difference between one young woman and another.

    George Bernard Shaw (1856–1950) *Major Barbara*, 1908, act III.

18. Girls like a man to be a bit on the bossy side.

    Frederick E. Smith, *633 Squadron*, 1956, ch. 14.

19. There is no more powerful aphrodisiac than success and power, nothing like the clink of gold to get a girl's hormones revving up.

    Wilbur Smith, *Hungry as the Sea*, 1978.

20. Sweet girl-graduates in their gold hair.

    Alfred, Lord Tennyson (1809–1892) *The Princess*, 1847, Prologue.

21. To nurse a blind ideal like a girl
    Methinks he seems no better than a girl.
    > Alfred, Lord Tennyson (1809–1892) *ibid.* part III.

22. I doubt, as you know, if the same kind of girl is suitable
    for engagements as for marriage.
    > H. G. Wells (1866–1946) *Select Conversations with an Uncle*, 1895.

49. Happiness

1. A man always thinks himself to be the source of his
   wife's happiness.
   > Anonymous.

2. All the young ladies . . . said . . . that a love match was
   the only thing for happiness.
   > Maria Edgeworth (1767–1849) *Castle Rackrent*, 1800, 'Continuation of Memoirs'.

3. The happiest women, like the happiest nations, have no
   history.
   > George Eliot (1819–1880) *The Mill on the Floss*, 1860, book VI, ch. 3.

4. The happiness of man is, 'I will'. The happiness of
   woman is, 'he will'.
   > Friedrich Nietzsche (1844–1900) *Thus Spake Zarathustra*, 1883–91, XVIII, 'Old and Young Women'.

5. That was always the trouble with women. They were
   never happy until they changed you.
   > Harold Robbins, *The Inheritors*, 1969, book 2, ch. 8.

6. He that hath a handsome wife, by other men is thought
   happy; 'tis a pleasure to look upon her, and be in her

company; but the husband is cloyed with her. We are never content with what we have.

John Selden (1584–1654) *Table-Talk*, 1689, CL, 'Wife'.

7. I sometimes think that a very poor man's wife is the happiest, because she does do everything.

Anthony Trollope (1815–1882) *The Small House at Allington*, 1864, ch. XV.

50. Hate

1. Of all the objects of hatred, a woman once loved is the most hateful.

Max Beerbohm (1872–1956) *Zuleika Dobson*, 1911, ch. XIII.

2. I never hated a man enough to give him his diamonds back.

Zsa Zsa Gabor. Quoted in L. J. Peter, *Peter's Quotations*.

3. Women have very little idea of how much men hate them.

Germaine Greer, *The Female Eunuch*, 1971, 'Loathing and Disgust'.

4. Women love to hate their best friends.

Pamela Kettle, *The Day of the Women*, 1969, ch. 1.

5. He hated her for his ineptitude.

Doris Lessing. *A Man and Two Women*, 1975.

6. I have been vexed to see husbands hate their wives only because they themselves do them wrong.

Michel de Montaigne (1533–1592) *Essays*, 1595, book III, ch. V.

7. Woman learns to hate in proportion as she forgets how to charm.

> Friedrich Nietzsche (1844–1900) *Beyond Good and Evil*, 1885, ch. VI, 84.

51. Home

1. A man's home is his hassle.

> Paul D. Arnold. Quoted in B. Rowe, *The Book of Quotes*.

2. Housework may not be Everest, but it is an adventure that awaits any man who wants to forge ahead and meet the challenges of unexplored territory.

> William R. Beer, *Househusbands*, 1983, p. xxi.

3. 'Home, sweet home' must surely have been invented by a bachelor.

> Samuel Butler (1835–1902) Attributed.

4. A man . . . is *so* in the way in the house.

> Elizabeth Gaskell (1810–1865) *Cranford*, 1853, ch. 1.

5. If the husband be not at home, there is nobody.

> George Herbert (1593–1633) *Jacula Prudentum*, 1651.

6. It is a sad home where the hen crows louder than the cock.

> Proverb.

7. A woman's place is in the home.

> Proverb.

8. If home is to have a greater lure than the tavern the wife must be at least as cheerful as the waitress.

> Phyllis Schlafly. Quoted in *The Sunday Times*, 17 January 1982.

9. Home is the girl's prison and the woman's workhouse.
    George Bernard Shaw (1856–1950) *Maxims for Revolutionists*, 1903.

52. Husbands

(*See also* Husbands and Wives)

1. A husband's place is in the wrong.
    Anonymous.

2. Do married men make the best husbands?
    Anonymous.

3. The majority of husbands remind me of an orang-utang trying to play the violin.
    Honoré de Balzac (1799–1850) *The Physiology of Marriage*, 1829.

4. Being a husband is a whole-time job.
    Arnold Bennett (1867–1931) *The Title*, 1918, act I.

5. When a man hath taken a new wife, he shall not go out to war, neither shall he be charged with any business; but he shall be free at home one year, and shall cheer up his wife which he hath taken.
    Bible, Authorized Version, Deuteronomy, 24: 5.

6. Oh! ye lords of ladies intellectual
    Inform us truly, have they not hen-pecked you all?
    Lord Byron (1788–1824) *Don Juan*, canto I, 1819, st. xxii.

7. It ought to be a source of satisfaction to many wives, even if they are of a jealous disposition, that their husbands show a healthy interest in other women.
    Henry Cecil, *Hunt the Slipper*, 1977, ch. 1.

8. Never join with your friend when he abuses his horse or his wife, unless the one is about to be *sold*, and the other to be *buried*.

    C. C. Colton (1780–1832) *Lacon*, 1820, vol. I, 376.

9. There is no creature perfectly civil but a husband. For in a little time he grows only rude to his wife, and that is the highest good breeding, for it begets his civility to other people.

    William Congreve (1670–1729) *Love for Love*, 1695, I. ii.

10. A man that is married, d'ye see, is no more like another man than a galley-slave is like one of us free sailors; he is chained to an oar all his life; and mayhap forced to tug a leaky vessel into the bargain.

    William Congreve (1670–1729) *ibid*. III. iii.

11. Every man plays the fool once in his life; but to marry is playing the fool all one's life long.

    William Congreve (1670–1729) *The Old Bachelor*, 1693, III. iv.

12. One good husband is worth two good wives; for the scarcer things are the more they're valued.

    Benjamin Franklin (1706–1790) *Poor Richard's Almanac*, 1742.

13. A good husband . . . avoideth all fondness (a sick love, to be praised in none, and pardoned only in the newly married) whereby more have wilfully betrayed their command than ever lost it by their wives' rebellion.

    Thomas Fuller (1608–1661) *The Holy and The Profane State*, 1642, 'The Good Husband'.

14. Husbands are horribly provoking; they know the frailty of the sex, and never fail to take advantage of our passions to make us expose ourselves by contradiction.

    John Gay (1685–1732) *Achilles*, 1733, act I.

15. A looker-on very often sees the oversights of those that are engag'd in the game; and of all mankind, according to my observations, a husband sees the least of what his wife is doing.

> John Gay (1685–1732) *The Distress'd Wife*,
> 1743, act I .

16. Husbands, like colts, are restive, and they require a long time to break 'em.

> John Gay (1685–1732) *Polly*, 1729, act I.

17. A husband without faults is a dangerous observer, he hath an eye so piercing, and seeth everything so plain, that it is exposed to his full censure.

> Lord Halifax (1633–1695) *Advice to a Daughter*, 1688.

18. He that tells his wife news is but newly married.

> George Herbert (1593–1633) *Jacula Prudentum*, 1651.

19. I should like to see any kind of man, distinguishable from a gorilla, that some good and even pretty woman could not shape a husband out of.

> Oliver Wendell Holmes (1809–1894) *The Professor at
> the Breakfast-Table*, 1860, ch. VII.

20. When women doubt most of their husband's loves,
> They are most loving. Husbands must take heed
> They give no gluts of kindness to their wives
> But use them like horses.

> Ben Jonson (1573–1637) *Every Man out of his Humour*,
> 1599, II. iv.

21. Often it's the trivial faults which most offend a husband.

> Juvenal (*c.* AD 60–*c.* 140) *Satires*, VI.

22. Speaking to or crying over a husband never did any good yet.

> Rudyard Kipling (1865–1936) *Plain Tales from the
> Hills*, 1888, 'Three and—an Extra'.

23. It is ridiculous to think you can spend your entire life with just one person. Three is about the right number. Yes, I imagine three husbands would do it.

Clare Boothe Luce. *Observer*, 'Sayings of the Week',
18 July 1981.

24. The husband is the attained and distained.

H. L. Mencken (1880–1956) *In Defence of Women*,
1922, 'Marriage'.

25. One can, to an almost laughable degree, infer what a man's wife is like, from his opinions about women in general.

John Stuart Mill (1806–1873) *The Subjection of
Women*, 1869, ch. I.

26. Though women do not complain of the power of husbands, each complains of her own husband, or the husbands of her friends.

John Stuart Mill (1806–1873) *ibid*. ch. III.

27. A wife is only a man's soup, but when a man sees other men who wish to dip their fingers in his soup he deeply resents it immediately.

Molière (1622–1673) *The School for Wives*,
1662, II. iv.

28. 'Tis the established custom [in Vienna] for every lady to have two husbands, one that bears the name, and another that performs the duties.

Lady Mary Wortley Montagu (1689–1762). Letter to
Lady Rich, 20 September 1716.

29. If there were no husbands, who would look after our mistresses?

George Moore (1852–1933) *Confessions of a Young
Man*, 1886.

30. A husband is what is left of the lover after the nerve has been extracted.

> Helen Rowland (1876–1950) *The Rubaiyat of a Bachelor*, 1915.

31. A young man married is a man that's marr'd.

> William Shakespeare (1564–1616) *All's Well That Ends Well*, 1602–4, II. iv.

32. A man ought to be able to be fond of his wife without making a fool of himself about her.

> George Bernard Shaw (1856–1950) *Candida*, 1898, act I.

33. A man as intimate with his own wife as a magistrate is with his clerk, or a prime minister with the leader of the opposition, is a man in ten thousand.

> George Bernard Shaw (1856–1950) *Getting Married*, 1908, Preface.

34. Except when the death of a man's wife occurs at such a time that he has to pay a stranger to discharge her household and parental duties until|he goes back to the cheaper plan of marrying again, it is very hard to convince him that his wife is a productive worker.

> George Bernard Shaw (1856–1950). Letter, 1895.

35. No man worth having is true to his wife, or can be true to his wife, or ever was, or ever will be so.

> Sir John Vanbrugh (1664–1726) *The Relapse*, 1697, III. ii.

36. A husband is just property, a mere draught-camel for her service.

> H. G. Wells (1866–1946) *Select Conversation with an Uncle*, 1895.

37.   If we men married the women we deserved, we should
      have a very bad time of it.
                        Oscar Wilde (1854–1900) *An Ideal Husband*,
                                                        1899, act IV.

38.   They are horribly tedious when they are good
      husbands, and abominably conceited when they are
      not.
                  Oscar Wilde (1854–1900) *A Woman of No Importance*,
                                                        1893, act II.

39.   All the unhappy marriages come from the husbands
      having brains. What good are brains to a man?
                        P. G. Wodehouse (1881–1975) *The Adventures of
                                                        Sally*, 1923.

40.   The *divine right* of husbands, like the divine right of
      kings, may, it is to be hoped, in this enlightened age, be
      contested without danger.
                  Mary Wollstonecraft (1759–1797) *A Vindication of the
                                        Rights of Woman*, 1792, ch. III.

53. Husbands and Wives

1.   *Nancy Astor*: Winston, if I were married to you, I'd put
      poison in your coffee.
      Winston Churchill: Nancy, if you were my wife, I'd drink
      it.
                        Nancy Astor (1879–1964); Winston Churchill
                        (1874–1965). Quoted in E. Langhorne,
                                        Nancy Astor and her Friends.

2.   It is often seen that bad husbands have very good wives;
      whether it be that it raiseth the price of their husband's
      kindness when it comes; or that the wives take a pride in
      their patience.
                        Francis Bacon (1561–1626) *Essays*, 1597, VIII, 'Of
                                        Marriage and Single Life'.

3. Wives, submit yourselves unto your own husbands, as
   unto the Lord. For the husband is the head of the wife,
   even as Christ is the head of the Church.
       Bible, Authorized Version, Ephesians, 5:22–3.

4. Belinda: Men grow such clowns when they are married.
   Bellmour: That they are fit for no company but their
   wives.
       William Congreve (1670–1729) *The Old Bachelor*,
       1693, V. v.

5. The calmest husbands make the stormiest wives.
       Thomas Dekker (*c*. 1570–*c*.1641) *The Honest Whore*,
       1604, part I, V. i.

6. The reason that husbands and wives do not understand
   each other is because they belong to different sexes.
       Dorothy Dix (1861–1951) Attributed.

7. He knows little, who will tell his wife all he knows.
       Thomas Fuller (1608–1661) *The Holy and The Profane
       State*, 1642, 'The Good Husband'.

8. Peachum: And how do you propose to live, child?
   Polly: Like other women sir, upon the industry of my
   husband.
       John Gay (1685–1732) *The Beggar's Opera*, 1728, I. x.

9. The husband's sullen, dogged, shy,
   The wife grows flippant in reply;
   He loves command and due restriction,
   And she as well likes contradiction;
   She never slavishly submits,
   She'll have her will, or have her fits;
   He this way tugs, she t'other way draws.
       John Gay (1685–1732) *Cupid, Hymen and Plutus*.

10. There are only about 20 murders a year in London and not all are serious—some are just husbands killing their wives.

> Commander G. H. Hatherill of Scotland Yard,
> *Observer*, 'Quotations of the Week',
> 21 February 1954.

11. In the husband wisdom, in the wife gentleness.

> George Herbert (1593–1633) *Jacula Prudentum*, 1651.

12. The hen should not crow in the presence of the cock.

> Molière (1622–1673) *The Learned Ladies*, 1672, V. iii.

13. A light wife doth make a heavy husband.

> William Shakespeare (1564–1616) *The Merchant of Venice*, 1596–97, V. i.

14. Thy husband is thy lord, thy life, thy keeper,
Thy head, thy sovereign.

> William Shakespeare (1564–1616) *The Taming of the Shrew*, 1593–94, V. ii.

15. What's the good of beating your wife unless there's a witness to prove it afterwards? You don't suppose a man beats his wife for the fun of it do you?

> George Bernard Shaw (1856–1950) *Getting Married*, 1908.

16. As the husband is, the wife is: thou art mated with a clown,
And the grossness of his nature will have to drag thee down.

> Alfred, Lord Tennyson (1809–1892) *Locksley Hall*, 1842.

17. Wives might be govern'd were not husbands fools.

> Sir John Vanbrugh (1664–1726) *The Provok'd Husband*, 1728, Epilogue.

18. It's most dangerous nowadays for a husband to pay any attention to his wife in public. It always makes people think that he beats her when they're alone. The world has grown suspicious of anything that looks like a happy married life.

> Oscar Wilde (1854–1900) *Lady Windermere's Fan*, 1892, act II.

19. Faithless husbands will make faithless wives.

> Mary Wollstonecraft (1759–1797) *A Vindication of the Rights of Woman*, 1792.

54. Illness

1. A sick headache is an affectation offering infinite resources. It has no symptoms, therefore it is the easiest of all maladies to simulate; all one has to do is to say simply 'I have a headache'. No living person can give a woman the lie if she chooses to make such a remark—her head defies both touch and observation.

> Honoré de Balzac (1799–1850) *The Physiology of Marriage*, 1829, book III, ch. XXVI.

2. By means of a headache a woman can drive her husband to despair. It seizes her when she likes, where she likes, for as long as she likes.

> Honoré de Balzac (1799–1850). *ibid.*

3. Hell hath no fury like a woman's corns.

> Nigel Rees, *Quote . . . Unquote 2*, 1980.

4. Dr Wilkinson dispels the myth that migraine sufferers are mainly to be found among the intellectual elite and says that in fact, migraine is about three times more common in women than men.

> *Sunderland Echo*—review of a Family Doctor Booklet on migraine, quoted in A. Veitch, *Naked Ape*.

55. Intelligence

1. Plenty of men have no objection to butterfly minds.
    Henry Cecil, *Brothers in Law*, 1955, ch. 4.

2. The man who thinks backwards is very frequently a woman.
    G. K. Chesterton (1874–1936) *A Miscellany of Men*, 1912, 'The Man Who Thinks Backwards'.

3. I'm not denyin' the women are foolish: God almighty made 'em to match the men.
    George Eliot (1819–1880) *Adam Bede*, 1859, ch. 53.

4. There is no female mind. The brain is not an organ of sex. As well speak of a female liver.
    Charlotte Perkins Gilman (1860–1935) *Women and Economics*, 1898, ch. VIII.

5. There is inequality in the sexes, and that for the better economy of the world the men, who were to be the lawgivers, had the larger share of reason bestowed upon them; by which means your sex is the better prepared for the compliance that is necessary for the better performance of those duties which seem to be most properly assigned to it.
    Lord Halifax (1633–1695) *Advice to a Daughter*, 1688.

6. Stupidity often saves a man from going mad.
    Oliver Wendell Holmes (1809–1894) *The Autocrat of the Breakfast-Table*, 1858, ch. II.

7. In men, the intellectual faculties exist more self-poised and self-directed, more independent of the rest of the character, than we ever find them in women, with whom talent, however predominant, is in a much greater degree modified by the sympathies and moral qualities.
    Anna Jameson (1797–1860) *Shakespeare's Heroines*, 1879, 'Portia'.

8. Women's thoughts are thus as useful in giving reality to those of thinking men, as men's thoughts in giving width and largeness to those of women.
    John Stuart Mill (1806–1873) *The Subjection of Women*, 1869, ch. III.

9. . . . the usual masculine disillusionment in discovering that a woman has a brain.
    Margaret Mitchell (1900–1949) *Gone with the Wind*, 1936, part IV, ch. 36.

10. Well, of course, you can't expect a silly little woman like me to understand men's affairs.
    Margaret Mitchell (1900–1949), *ibid.*

11. It is too great an insult to our sex to insist that the extent of our intelligence is an opinion of a petticoat.
    Molière (1622–1673) *The Learned Ladies*, 1672, III. ii.

12. Should a woman of a more cultivated understanding endeavour to give a rational turn to the conversation, the common source of consolation is that such women seldom get husbands.
    Mary Wollstonecraft (1759–1797) *A Vindication of the Rights of Woman*, 1792, ch. XII.

56. Intrigue

1. It must be a plot because there's a woman in't.
    George Farquhar (1678–1707) *The Beaux Stratagem*, 1707, IV. i.

2. I begin to fancy there may be as much pleasure in carrying on another body's intrigue as one's own. This at least is certain, it exercises almost all the entertaining faculties of a woman. For there's employment for hypocrisy, invention, deceit, flattery, mischief and lying.
    Sir John Vanbrugh (1664–1726) *The Relapse*, 1697, III. ii.

57. Intuition

1. Intuitions are the natural resource of a type of mind which is not adept at reasoning.
    > Arnold Bennett (1867–1931) *Our Women*,
    > 1920, ch. IV.

2. A woman's intuition has often proved truer than man's arrogant assumption of superior knowledge.
    > Mahatma Gandhi (1869–1948) Attributed.

3. Women's intuition is the result of millions of years of not thinking.
    > Rupert Hughes (1872–1956). Quoted in N. Bentley
    > and E. Esar, *The Treasury of Humorous Quotations*.

4. A woman's guess is much more accurate than a man's certainty.
    > Rudyard Kipling (1865–1936) *Plain Tales from the*
    > *Hills*, 1888, 'Three and—an Extra'.

58. Jealousy

1. It is impossible for a jealous man to be thoroughly cured of his suspicions.
    > Joseph Addison (1672–1719) *The Spectator*, no. 170,
    > 14 September 1711.

2. When the effects of female jealousy do not appear openly in their proper colours of rage and fury, we may suspect that mischievous passion to be at work privately, and attempting to undermine what it doth not attack above ground.
    > Henry Fielding (1707–1754) *Tom Jones*, 1749,
    > book XV, ch. I.

3. What a wretched, mean, contemptible figure is a jealous woman!
    > John Gay (1685–1732) *Achilles*, 1733, act I.

4. A jealous woman believes everything her passion suggests.

> John Gay (1685–1732) *The Beggar's Opera*,
> 1728, II. ix.

5. Women, by their jealousies, put one in mind of doing that which otherwise we should never think of.

> John Gay (1685–1732) *Polly*, 1729, act I.

6. Coquettes are jealous of their lovers so that they can conceal their envy of other women.

> François, Duc de La Rochefoucauld (1613–1680)
> *Maxims, 1678.*

7. Sometimes a husband enjoys having a jealous wife; he hears what he loves being talked about all the time.

> François, Duc de la Rochefoucauld (1613–1680) *ibid.*

8. It's matrimonial suicide to be jealous when you have a really good reason.

> Clare Boothe Luce, *The Women*, 1937, act III.

9. To give women the same counsel against jealousy would be so much time lost; their very being is so made up of suspicion, vanity, and curiosity, that to cure them by any legitimate way is not to be hoped.

> Michel de Montaigne (1533–1592) *Essays*, 1595,
> book III, ch. V.

10. All jealous women are mad.

> Arthur Wing Pinero (1855–1934) *The Second Mrs
> Tanqueray*, 1893, act II.

11. For story and experience tell us,
    That man grows old and woman jealous.

> Matthew Prior (1664–1721) *Alma*, 1718, canto II, l.65.

12. The venom clamours of a jealous woman
    Poison more deadly than a mad dog's tooth.
    William Shakespeare (1564–1616) *The Comedy of Errors*, 1592–93, V. i.

13. *Mrs Allonby*: Curious thing, plain women are always jealous of their husbands, beautiful women never are! *Lord Illingworth*: Beautiful women never have time. They are always so jealous of other people's husbands.
    Oscar Wilde (1854–1900) *A Woman of No Importance*, 1893, act I.

59. Jewellery

1. Have you ever noticed, Harry, that many jewels make women either incredibly fat or incredibly thin.
   J. M. Barrie (1860–1937) *The Twelve-Pound Look*, 1910.

2. Don't ever wear artistic jewellery; it wrecks a woman's reputation.
   Colette (1873–1954) *Gigi*, 1945.

3. Kissing your hand may make you feel very very good but a diamond and a sapphire bracelet lasts forever.
   Anita Loos (1893–1981) *Gentlemen Prefer Blondes*, 1925, ch. 4.

4. Comparing man and woman generally, one may say that woman would not have the genius for adornment, if she had not the instinct for the *secondary* role.
   Friedrich Nietzsche (1844–1900) *Beyond Good and Evil*, 1885, ch. IV, 145.

5. Win her with gifts, if she respect not words;
   Dumb jewels often, in their silent kind,
   More than quick words do move a woman's mind.
   William Shakespeare (1564–1616) *Two Gentlemen of Verona*, 1594–95, III. i.

60. Kissing

1. Some women blush when they are kissed; some call for the police; some swear; some bite. But the worst are those who laugh.

   Anonymous. Quoted in H. L. Mencken, *Dictionary of Quotations*.

2. When the girl you kiss gives as good as you give, you are not getting firsts.

   Anonymous, *ibid*.

3. I'll scream if you touch me—exclaimed a pert miss,
   When her lover attempted an innocent kiss.
   But when he gave up and made ready to go,
   The damsel cried louder—I'll scream till you do.

   Martial (*c.* AD 40–*c.* 104) *Epigrams*, trans. Pott and Wright, book IV, xlviii.

4. When women kiss it always reminds one of prize-fighters shaking hands.

   H. L. Mencken (1880–1956) *Sententiæ*, in A. Cooke, *The Vintage Mencken*.

5. A kiss without a moustache, they said then, is like an egg without salt.

   Jean-Paul Sartre (1905–1980) *Words*, 1964, part I.

61. The Law

1. Were women permitted to plead in courts of judicature, I am persuaded they would carry the eloquence of the bar to greater heights than it has yet arrived at. If any one doubt this, let him but be present at those debates which frequently arise among the ladies of the British fishery.

   Joseph Addison (1672–1719) *The Spectator*, no. 247, 13 December 1711.

2. A woman's income chargeable to income tax shall . . . (for any year) during which she is a married woman living with her husband be deemed for income tax purposes to be his income and not to be her income.

> Anonymous. UK *Income and Corporation Taxes Act* 1970, sect. 37.

3. I make a just complaint to the great wisdom and sagacity of our law, which refuses to admit the evidence of a wife for or against her husband. This, says a certain learned author . . . would be the means of creating an eternal dissension between them. It would, indeed, be the means of perjury, and of whipping, fining, imprisoning, transporting and hanging.

> Henry Fielding (1707–1754) *Tom Jones*, 1749, book I, ch. V.

4. Nature has given women so much power that the law has very wisely given them little.

> Samuel Johnson (1709–1784) Letter to John Taylor, 18 August 1763.

5. There has hardly been a court case in which the litigation was not started by a woman.

> Juvenal (*c.* AD 60–*c.* 140) *Satires*, VI.

6. By the old laws of England, the husband was called the *lord* of the wife; he was literally regarded as her sovereign, inasmuch that the murder of a man by his wife was called treason (*petty* as distinguished from *high* treason).

> John Stuart Mill (1806–1873) *The Subjection of Women*, 1869, ch. II.

7. Even if every woman were a wife, and if every wife ought to be a slave, all the more would these slaves stand in need of legal protection: and we know what legal protection the slaves have, where the laws are made by their masters.

> John Stuart Mill (1806–1873) *ibid.* ch. III.

8. The laws respecting woman . . . make an absurd unit of a man and his wife; and then, by the easy transition of only considering him as responsible, she is reduced to a mere cipher.

    Mary Wollstonecraft (1759–1797) *A Vindication of the Rights of Woman*, 1792, ch. IX.

62. Literature

1. It is said that every man has the stuff in him of one good novel. I doubt it; but I do not deny that every man has the stuff in him of one original book about women. And why more men—even philosophers and scientists—do not write books about women and more women books about men, I cannot imagine.

    Arnold Bennett (1867–1931) *Our Women*, 1920, ch.1, 'The Perils of Writing about Women'.

2. A female pen calls female virtue forth,
    And fairly shews to man her sex's worth.
    How apt their wit, their constancy—how true.

    Hannah Cowley (1743–1809) *A Bold Stroke for a Husband*, 1784, Prologue.

3. Alas, a woman that attempts the pen
    Such an intruder on the rights of men.

    Ann Finch, Countess of Winchilsea (1661–1720).
    Quoted in L. Spender, *Intruders On the Rights of Men*.

4. We know of course that women are habitually constipated, but to represent them in fiction as being altogether devoid of a back passage seems to me really an excess of chivalry.

    W. Somerset Maugham (1874–1966) *Cakes and Ale*, 1930, ch. 11.

5.   The greater part of what women write about women is
     mere sycophancy to men.
                    John Stuart Mill (1806–1873), *The Subjection of
                                           Women*, 1869, ch. I.

6.   There is one *human* consideration which would perhaps
     more effectually tend to damp in an aspiring woman
     the ardours of literary vanity ... she will have to
     encounter the mortifying circumstance of having her
     sex always taken into account, and her highest exertions
     will probably be received with the approbation *that it is
     really extraordinary for a woman.*
                    Hannah More (1745–1833) *Strictures on the Modern
                         System of Female Education*, 1799, ch. XIV.

7.   Pomfret hated women novelists. In his opinion,
     everything written by a woman was bad. Pomfret had
     very fixed ideas about a woman's duties and writing
     books was not one of them. One of his favourite forms
     of self-torture was to take a book by one of the more
     popular women novelists and read it slowly word by
     word, suffering as much as he could in the process.
                    Eric Williams, *The Wooden Horse*, 1949, ch. VI.

63. Love

1.   Women wish to be loved without a why or a wherefore;
     not because they are pretty, or good, or well bred, or
     graceful, or intelligent, but because they are themselves.
                    Henri-Frédéric Amiel (1821–1881) *Journal*,
                                            17 March 1868.

2.   The more a man loves, the more he suffers.
                    Henri-Frédéric Amiel (1821–1881) *ibid*.
                                        26 December 1868.

3.   Modern love is a many-gendered thing.
                                            Anonymous.

4.   A woman, O my friends, has one desire—
     To see secure, to live with, those she loves.
             Matthew Arnold (1822–1888) *Merope*, 1858, p.37.

5.   Woman's love is writ in water!
     Woman's faith is traced in sand!
             William Aytoun (1813–1865) *Charles Edward at*
                             Versailles, 1849 (*see also* 64.2).

6.   Love's so different with men!
             Robert Browning (1812–1889) *In a Year*, IX.

7.   Man's love is of man's life a thing apart,
     'Tis woman's whole existence.
                     Lord Byron (1788–1824) *Don Juan*,
                             canto I, 1819, st. cxciv.

8.   Alas! the love of women! it is known
     To be a lovely and a fearful thing.
                     Lord Byron (1788–1824) *ibid*.
                             canto II, 1819, st. cxcix.

9.   In her first passion woman loves her lover,
     In all the others all she loves is love.
                     Lord Byron (1788–1824) *ibid*. canto III,
                             1821, st. iii (*see also* 63.23).

10. Women generally consider consequences in love,
     seldom in resentment.
             C. C. Colton (1780–1832) *Lacon*, 1820, vol. I, 516.

11. If you cannot inspire a woman with love of you, fill her
     above the brim with love of herself;—all that runs over
     will be yours.
             C. C. Colton (1780–1832) *ibid*. vol. II, 89.

12. I believe the baggage loves me; for the she never speaks well of me herself, nor suffers anybody else to rail at me.

> William Congreve (1670–1729) *The Old Bachelor*, 1693, I. i.

13. Poor love is lost in men's capacious minds,
     In ours, it fills up all the room it finds.

> John Crowne (*c*. 1640–*c*. 1703) *Thyestes*, 1681.

14. It's very dangerous if you keep love letters from someone who is not now your husband.

> Diana Dors, *Observer*, 'Sayings of the Week', 15 September 1980.

15. Women know no perfect love:
     Loving the strong, they can forsake the strong;
     Man clings because the being whom he loves
     Is weak and needs him.

> George Eliot (1819–1880) *The Spanish Gypsy*, 1868, book III.

16. How a little love and good company improves a woman.

> George Farquhar (1678–1707) *The Beaux Stratagem*, 1707, IV. i.

17. Men are often blind to the passions of women: but every woman is as quick-sighted as a hawk on these occasions.

> Henry Fielding (1707–1754) *Amelia*, 1751, book II, ch. II.

18. The discourse turned at present on love; and Mr Nightingale expressed many of those warm, generous, and disinterested sentiments upon this subject which wise and sober men call romantic, but which wise and sober women generally regard in a better light.

> Henry Fielding (1707–1754) *Tom Jones*, 1749, book XIII, ch. V.

19. A man in love is incomplete until he has married. Then he's finished.

> Zsa Zsa Gabor. Quoted in *Newsweek*, 28 March 1960.

20. Outside of love there is no life for woman.

> Remy de Gourmont (1858–1915) *The Young Lady of Today*.

21. All excitements run to love in women of a certain—let us not say age, but youth.

> Oliver Wendell Holmes (1809–1894) *The Professor at the Breakfast-Table*, 1860, ch. VII.

22. Women in love forgive large indiscretions more easily than small infidelities.

> François, Duc de la Rochefoucauld (1613–1680) *Maxims*, 1678.

23. In their first love women love the lover, and in the others they are in love with love.

> François, Duc de La Rochefoucauld (1613–1680) *ibid*. (*see also* 63.9).

24. Nowadays you are told: 'You must love one man only'. It is as if someone were to force me to eat turkey only all my life.

> Guy de Maupassant (1850–1893) *A Grandmother's Advice*.

25. A silly woman knows more about these things [love] than the cleverest man.

> Molière (1622–1673) *The School for Wives*, 1662, V. iv.

26. Love a woman! you're an ass,
'Tis a most insipid passion;
To choose out for your happiness
The silliest part of God's creation.

> Earl of Rochester (1647–1680) *Song*.

27.   Ophelia: 'Tis brief, my lord.
      Hamlet: As woman's love.
>   William Shakespeare (1564–1616) *Hamlet*,
>   1599–1600, II. ii.

28.   Cupid is a knavish cad,
      Thus to make poor females mad.
>   William Shakespeare (1564–1616) *A Midsummer
>   Night's Dream*, 1596, IV. ii.

29.   I do much wonder that one man, seeing how much
      another man is a fool, when he dedicates his behaviours
      to love, will, after he hath laughed at such shallow
      follies in others, become the argument of his own scorn
      by falling in love.
>   William Shakespeare (1564–1616) *Much Ado About
>   Nothing*, 1598–99, II. iii.

30.   They love least that let men know their love.
>   William Shakespeare (1564–1616) *Two Gentlemen of
>   Verona*, 1594–95, I. ii.

31.   A man's power of love and admiration is like any other
      of his powers: he has to throw it away many times
      before he learns what is really worthy of it.
>   George Bernard Shaw (1856–1950) *You Never Can
>   Tell*, 1898, act III.

32.   I do not know whether women ever love. I rather doubt
      it: they pity a man, *mother* him, delight in making him
      love them; but I always suspect that their tenderness is
      deepened by their remorse for being unable to love
      him.
>   George Bernard Shaw (1856–1950). Letter to Ellen
>   Terry, 6 April 1896.

33.   In the spring a young man's fancy lightly turns to
      thoughts of love.
>   Alfred, Lord Tennyson (1809–1892) *Locksley
>   Hall*, 1842.

34.   *Belinda*: When a man is really in love, he looks so unsufferably silly that though a woman liked him well enough before, she has then much ado to endure the sight of him . . .
Lady Brute: Well, I own now, I'm well enough pleased to see a man look like an ass for me.
Belinda: Ay I'm pleased he should look like an ass too—that is, I'm pleased with myself for making him look so.

> Sir John Vanbrugh (1664–1726) *The Provok'd Wife*,
> 1698, III. iii.

35.   Once a woman has given you her heart you can never get rid of the rest of her body.

> Sir John Vanbrugh (1664–1726) *The Relapse*,
> 1697, III. i.

36.   He who loves and runs away may live to love another day.

> Carolyn Wells (1862–1942). Quoted in N. Bentley
> and E. Esar, *The Treasury of Humorous Quotations*.

37.   Love is a mood—no more—to man
And love to woman is life or death.

> Ella Wheeler Wilcox (1850–1919) *Blind*.

38.   I suppose that when a man has once loved a woman, he will do anything for her, except continue to love her?

> Oscar Wilde (1854–1900) *An Ideal Husband*,
> 1899, act III.

39.   A man can be happy with any woman, as long as he does not love her.

> Oscar Wilde (1854–1900) *The Picture of Dorian Gray*,
> 1891, ch. 15.

40.   Women love us for our defects. If we have enough of them they will forgive us everything, even our intellects.

> Oscar Wilde (1854–1900) *ibid*.

41. Men always want to be a woman's first love. That is their clumsy vanity. We women have a more subtle instinct about things. What we like is to be a man's last romance.

> Oscar Wilde (1854–1900) *A Woman of No Importance*,
> 1893, act II.

42. Women of quality are so civil that you can hardly distinguish love from good breeding, and a man is often mistaken.

> William Wycherley (1640–1716) *The Country Wife*,
> 1675, I. i.

64. Lovers

1. I've seen your stormy seas and stormy women,
    And pity lovers rather more than seamen.

> Lord Byron (1788–1824) *Don Juan*, canto VI,
> 1821, st. iii.

2. What a girl promises her lover ought to be written on water, or written on air.

> Catullus (87–c. 54 BC) *Poems*, no. LXX (*see also* 63.5).

3. I think it will do well enough, if the husband be out of the way, for the wife to show her fondness and impatience of his absence by choosing a lover as like him as she can; and what is unlike, she may help out with her own fancy.

> William Congreve (1670–1729) *The Old Bachelor*,
> 1693, I. i.

4. The fair-sex reigns with greater tyranny over lovers than husbands.

> Sir Richard Steele (1672–1729) *The Spectator*, no. 486,
> 17 September 1712.

5.   I doubt whether any girl would be satisfied with her lover's mind if she knew the whole of it.

> Anthony Trollope (1815–1882) *The Small House at Allington*, 1864, ch. 4.

65. Marriage

1.   Did you ever hear of a woman who had power over a man, when she was his wife, that had none while she was his mistress! Oh! there's nothing in the world improves a man in his complaisance like marriage.

> Joseph Addison (1672–1719) *The Drummer*, 1716, I. i.

2.   Too long has marriage, in this tasteless age,
With ill-bred raillery supply'd the stage;
No little scribbler is of wit so bare,
But has his fling at the poor wedded pair.

> Joseph Addison (1672–1719) *ibid*. Epilogue.

3.   It is very usual for those who have been severe upon marriage, in some part or other of their lives to enter into the fraternity which they have ridiculed, and to see their raillery return upon their own heads. I scarce ever knew a woman-hater that did not sooner or later pay for it.

> Joseph Addison (1672–1719) *The Spectator*, no. 530, 7 November 1712.

4.   Before marriage a man will lie awake thinking of what you have said. After marriage he will fall asleep before you have finished saying it.

> Anonymous.

5.   If you want to be happy for a day, get drunk. If you want to be happy for a week, get married. But if you want to be happy for life, go fishing.

> Anonymous.

6. A person who believes she is only complete as part of a twosome believes she is only half a person.

    Anonymous.

7. Very few people are cut out for marriage—and they are all women.

    Anonymous.

8. You could try marrying a witch and hoping that she will turn into a princess—most men experience the opposite.

    Anonymous.

9. A lady's imagination is very rapid; it jumps from admiration to love, from love to matrimony, in a moment.

    Jane Austen (1775–1817) *Pride and Prejudice*, 1813, ch. 6.

10. Marriage in my experience was a ring drawn around a man's life by the radius of his natural limitations. On marrying him you went inside and stayed there, forswearing all limitations of your own.

    Mary Austin (1868–1934) *A Woman of Genius*, 1912, book IV, ch. IX.

11. He was reputed one of the wise men, that made answer to the question when a man should marry?—'A young man not yet, an elder man not at all.'

    Francis Bacon (1561–1626) *Essays*, 1597, VIII, 'Of Marriage and Single Life'.

12. Marriage, *n*. The state or condition of a community consisting of a master, a mistress and two slaves, making in all, two.

    Ambrose Bierce (1842–*c*. 1914) *The Devil's Dictionary*, 1911.

13.   Marriage is a duel to the death, which no man of honour
      should decline.
         G. K. Chesterton (1874–1936) *Manalive*, 1912, ch. IV.

14.   The two extremes appear like man and wife,
      Coupled together for the sake of strife.
                        Charles Churchill (1731–1764) *The Rosciad*,
                                                 1750, l. 1,005.

15.   Though marriage makes man and wife one flesh, it
      leaves them still two fools; and they become more
      conspicuous by setting off one another.
               William Congreve (1670–1729) *The Double-Dealer*,
                                                 1694, II. i.

16.   Marriage indeed may qualify the fury of his passion, but
      it rarely mends a man's manners.
                     William Congreve (1670–1729) *Love for Love*,
                                                 1695, I. ii.

17.   Sir Sampson is enraged, and talks desperately of
      committing matrimony himself.
                     William Congreve (1670–1729) *ibid*. IV. iii.

18.   *Sharper*: Thus grief still treads upon the heels of
      pleasure;
      Married in haste, we may repent at leisure.
      Setter: Some by experience find those words misplaced
      At leisure married, they repent in haste.
                  William Congreve (1670–1729) *The Old Bachelor*,
                                                 1693, V. iii.

19.   *Heartwell*: I have once escaped, and when I wed again,
      may she be as ugly as an old bawd.
      Vainlove: Ill-natured as an old maid—
      Bellmour: Wanton as a young widow—
      Sharper: And jealous as a barren wife.
      Heartwell: Agreed.
                     William Congreve (1670–1729) *ibid*. V. v.

20. I have always thought that every woman should marry and no man.
    Benjamin Disraeli (1804–1881) *Lothair*, 1870, ch. 30.

21. A woman dictates before marriage in order that she might have an appetite for submission afterwards.
    George Eliot (1819–1880) *Middlemarch*, 1871, book I, ch. 9.

22. A bachelor was saying, *Next to no wife, a good wife is best. Nay*, said a gentlewoman, *next to a good wife, no wife is the best*.
    Thomas Fuller (1608–1661) *The Holy and the Profane State*, 1642, 'Marriage'.

23. Marry your son when you will; your daughter when you can.
    George Herbert (1593–1633) *Jacula Prudentum*, 1651.

24. Men are always doomed to be duped . . . They are always wooing goddesses, and marrying mere mortals.
    Washington Irving (1783–1859) *Bracebridge Hall*, 1822.

25. A gentleman who had been very unhappy in marriage, married immediately after his wife died: Johnson said, it was the triumph of hope over experience.
    Samuel Johnson (1709–1784) *Boswell's Life*, 1770.

26. Men know that women are an over-match for them, and therefore they choose the weakest or most ignorant.
    Samuel Johnson (1709–1784) *ibid*. 19 September 1773.

27. All women should marry younger men. After all, men reach their sexual prime at 19 and women can reach it at 90.
    Penelope Keith, *Observer*, 'Sayings of the Week', 16 October 1983.

28. I think marriage is shocking. How can one dream of lying naked next to a man.

>   Molière (1622–1673) *The Learned Ladies*, 1672, I. iv.

29. I will marry a silly girl so that I will not be made a fool of.

>   Molière (1622–1673) *The School for Wives*, 1662, I. i.

30. 'Twas a happy marriage betwixt a blind wife and a deaf husband.

>   Michel de Montaigne (1533–1592) *Essays*, 1595,
>   book III, ch. V.

31. Marriage is like pleading guilty to an indefinite sentence. Without parole.

>   John Mortimer, *The Trials of Rumpole*, 1979,
>   'Rumpole and the Man of God'.

32. It is, of course, highly paradoxical that placement in a structure of subordination (marriage) should be regarded as an achievement worth fighting one's sisters for.

>   Ann Oakley, *Subject Women*, 1981, ch. 12.

33. No one asks a man how his marriage survives if he's away a lot.

>   Angela Rippon, *Observer*, 'Sayings of the Week',
>   27 September 1981.

34. It does not much signify whom one marries, for one is sure to find next morning that it was someone else.

>   Samuel Rogers (1763–1855) *Table Talk*, 1856.

35. When a girl marries she exchanges the attention of many men for the inattention of one.

>   Helen Rowland (1876–1950). Quoted in J. Cooper
>   and T. Hartman, *Violets and Vinegar*.

36. In olden times sacrifices were made at the altar—a custom which is still continued.
    Helen Rowland (1876–1950). Quoted in B. House,
    From Eve On.

37. Men are April when they woo, December when they wed: maids are May when they are maids, but the sky changes when they are wives.
    William Shakespeare (1564–1616) *As you Like It,*
    1596–1600, IV. i.

38. The whole world is strewn with snares, traps, gins, and pitfalls for the capture of men by women.
    George Bernard Shaw (1856–1950) *Man and Superman*, 1903, Epistle Dedicatory.

39. It is a woman's business to get married as soon as possible, and a man's to keep unmarried as long as he can.
    George Bernard Shaw (1856–1950) *ibid.* act II.

40. I am glad I am not a man, for if I were I should be obliged to marry a woman.
    Mme. de Staël (1766–1817) Attributed.

41. The only guy that shouldn't have nothing to do with picking out a wife is the guy that's going to marry her. That's a fact. It's a fact that if he's left alone a guy practically always marries the wrong kind of dame.
    John Steinbeck (1902–1968) *Sweet Thursday,*
    1954, ch. 11.

42. Marriage is a step so grave and decisive that it attracts light-headed, variable men by its very awfulness.
    Robert Louis Stevenson (1850–1894) *Virginibus Puerisque*, 1881, I.

43. The man who should hold back from marrige is in the same case with him who runs away from a battle.
    Robert Louis Stevenson (1850–1894) *ibid.* II.

44.   The reason why so few marriages are happy, is, because young ladies spend their time in making *nets*, and not in making *cages*.

> Jonathan Swift (1667–1745) *Thoughts on Various Subjects*, 1711.

45.   I don't want to be the rose on my husband's lapel.

> Margaret Trudeau. Attributed.

46.   The woman's well enough, she has no vice that I know of, but she's a wife and—damn a wife! If I were married to a hogshead of claret, matrimony would make me hate it.

> Sir John Vanbrugh (1664–1726) *The Provok'd Wife*, 1698, II. i.

47.   There's nothing in the world like the devotion of a married woman. It's a thing no married man knows anything about.

> Oscar Wilde (1854–1900) *Lady Windermere's Fan*, 1892, act III.

48.   When a woman marries again it is because she detested her first husband. When a man marries again it is because he adored his first wife. Women try their luck; men risk theirs.

> Oscar Wilde (1854–1900) *The Picture of Dorian Gray*, 1891, ch. XV.

49.   More marriages are ruined nowadays by the common sense of the husband than by anything else. How can a woman be expected to be happy with a man who insists on treating her as if she were a perfectly rational being?

> Oscar Wilde (1854–1900) *A Woman of No Importance*, 1893, act II.

50.   Men marry because they are tired; women because they are curious. Both are disappointed.

> Oscar Wilde (1854–1900) *ibid.* act III.

51. Marriage is a bribe to make a housekeeper think she's a householder.
> Thornton Wilder (1897–1975) *The Matchmaker*,
> 1954, act I.

52. I may be told that a number of women are not slaves in the marriage state. True, but then they become tyrants; for it is not rational freedom, but a lawless kind of power, resembling the authority exercised by the favourites of absolute monarchs.
> Mary Wollstonecraft (1759–1797) *A Vindication of the*
> *Rights of Woman*, 1792, ch. XI.

53. 'Tis my maxim he's a fool that marries, but he's greater that does not marry a fool. What is wit in a wife for, but to make a man a cuckold?
> William Wycherley (1640–1716) *The Country Wife*,
> 1675, I. i.

54. The woman that marries to love better will be as much mistaken as the wencher who marries to live better.
> William Wycherley (1640–1716) *ibid.* IV. i.

66. Men

1. You are a man. You rush on your destruction.
> Joseph Addison (1672–1719) *Cato*, 1721, II. ii.

2. It is a man's world.
> Anonymous.

3. Women have many faults,
   Men have only two:
   Everything they say,
   And everything they do.
> Anonymous.

4.   I blush for our sex.
      Men *will* have it we are tricky and sly . . .
          Aristophanes (*c.* 448–*c.* 388 BC) *Lysistrata*, 411 BC.

5.   Wheresoe'er men are, there is grief.
          Matthew Arnold (1822–1888) *Merope*, 1858, p. 72.

6.   'You can talk all you want to', Cecelia asseverated,
      'about men being the natural provider. I've noticed he
      don't work at the job much without he's gettin'
      something out of it.'
          Mary Austin (1868–1934) *A Woman of Genius*, 1912,
                                              book III, ch. I.

7.   Men are nervous of remarkable women.
          J. M. Barrie (1860–1937) *What Every Woman Knows*,
                                              1908, act I.

8.   Men have a perfect passion for being exactly like other
      men—not merely in clothes, but in everything.
          Arnold Bennett (1867–1931) *Self and Self-Management*,
                      1911, 'The Meaning of Frocks'.

9.   Male, *n.* A member of the unconsidered, or negligible
      sex. The male of the human race is commonly known
      (to the female) as Mere Man. The genus has two
      varieties: good providers and bad providers.
          Ambrose Bierce (1842–*c.* 1914) *The Devil's
                                              Dictionary*, 1911.

10.   The standard English male thinks of a woman like an
      umbrella. It opens up when he wants, accompanies him
      when he wishes and can be put aside when he wants.
      But it is always there ready for use. When the umbrella
      says hey, I'm a person, the 'owner' feels impelled to get
      it under control and shut it up in some other way.
          Paul Brown. Quoted in Suzanne Lowry, *The
                                              Guilt Cage*.

11. Men are the sport of circumstances, when
    The circumstances seem the sport of men.
    > Lord Byron (1788–1824) *Don Juan*, canto V,
    > 1824, st. xvii.

12. Why is it you can never look with indifference at a
    woman unless she is yours?
    > Anton Chekhov (1860–1904) *Uncle Vanya*,
    > 1897, act I.

13. It *is* a man's world, and I've had to behave like a man
    because I've been up against them. I've been shaped by
    them, guided by them and manipulated by them. Yes,
    that's it, *man*-ipulated.
    > Diana Dors. Quoted in *The Sunday Times*,
    > 17 January 1982.

14. Men are but children of a larger growth.
    > John Dryden (1631–1700) *All for Love*, 1678, IV. i.

15. Man is but man; unconstant still and various
    There's no tomorrow in him, like today.
    > John Dryden (1631–1700) *Cleomenes*, 1692, III. i.

16. Men's men: gentle or simple, they're much of a
    muchness.
    > George Eliot (1819–1880) *Daniel Deronda*, 1876,
    > book IV, ch. 31.

17. In certain men, digestion and sex absorb the vital force,
    and the stronger these are, the individual is so much
    weaker.
    > Ralph Waldo Emerson (1803–1882) *The Conduct of
    > Life*, 1860, 'Fate'.

18. Man can never tell woman what her duties are: he will
    certainly end in describing a man in female attire.
    > Ralph Waldo Emerson (1803–1882) *Journal*, 1843.

19.   How—in a world where you're expected to be
sympathetic, sensitive, and split half the household
chores—how do you remain a 'Real Man'?
> Bruce Feirstein, *Real Men Don't Eat Quiche*,
> 1982, Introduction.

20.   *Anti-feminist*: I always thought women were meant to
be kissable, cuddly and sweet smelling.
Mrs Fenwick: That's what I thought of men, and I hope
for your sake, that you haven't been disappointed as
many times as I've been.
> Millicent Fenwick. Quoted in *The Times*,
> 3 November 1982.

21.   . . . man's capacity for putting woman on a pedestal and
at the same time trampling her underfoot.
> Eva Figes, *Patriarchal Attitudes*, 1970, ch. 1.

22.   Men love war because it allows them to look serious.
Because they imagine it is the one thing that stops
women laughing at them.
> John Fowles, *The Magus*, revised version, 1977.

23.   Surely men, contrary to iron, are worst to be wrought
upon when they are hot; and are far more tractable in
cold blood.
> Thomas Fuller (1608–1661) *The Holy and the Profane
> State*, 1642, 'The Good Wife'.

24.   Macho does not prove mucho.
> Zsa Zsa Gabor. Quoted in J. Green, *A Dictionary of
> Contemporary Quotations*.

25.   Mistress and wife can well supply his need,
A miss for pleasure, and a wife for breed.
> John Gay (1685–1732) *The Toilette*.

26.   Man's a ribald—man's a rake,
Man is nature's sole mistake!
> Sir W. S. Gilbert (1836–1911) *Princess Ida*, 1884, act II.

27. Most men who rail against women are railing at one woman only.

> Remy de Gourmont (1858–1915). Quoted in W. H. Auden and L. Kronenberger, *The Faber Book of Aphorisms.*

28. Men are like buses. If you miss one, there's always another round the corner. But don't get caught at the wrong stop.

> Wendy Henry, *Observer*, 'Sayings of the Week', 30 January, 1983.

29. When a man sleeps, his head is in his stomach.

> George Herbert (1593–1633) *Jacula Prudentum*, 1651.

30. Marriage, Sir, is much more necessary to a man than to a woman; for he is much less able to supply himself with domestic comforts.

> Samuel Johnson (1709–1784) *Boswell's Life*, 25 March 1776.

31. Whilst men wish to conquer women at large, they'll accept one special woman as a token, the better to subdue the multitudes!

> Erica Jong, *Fanny*, 1980, book III, ch. XI.

32. Love no man. Trust no man. Speak ill of no man to his face: nor well of any man behind his back.

> Ben Jonson (1573–1637) *Every Man out of his Humour*, 1599, III. iv.

33. There is nothing that men love better, or manage worse, than their lives.

> Jean de La Bruyère (1645–1696) *Characters*, 1688, 'Of Men', 34.

34. Most men spend the best part of their lives making the remaining part wretched.

> Jean de La Bruyère (1645–1696) *ibid.* 102.

35.   It is easier to know men in general than one man in
      particular.

> François, Duc de La Rochefoucauld (1613–1680)
> *Maxims*, 1678.

36.   Little is needed to make the wise happy; nothing can
      make a fool contented: this is why almost all men are
      miserable.

> François, Duc de La Rochefoucauld (1613–1680) *ibid.*

37.   Men have an extraordinarily erroneous opinion of their
      position in nature; and the error is ineradicable.

> W. Somerset Maugham (1874–1966) *A Writer's
> Notebook*, 1896.

38.   And man! ... Man? ... What a horrible animal,
      wicked, proud and disgusting.

> Guy de Maupassant (1850–1893) *A Divorce Case.*

39.   All that I have done in marrying her is to obey this
      senseless urge that drives us towards the female.

> Guy de Maupassant (1850–1893) *ibid.*

40.   Masculinity and stupidity are often indistinguishable.

> H. L. Mencken (1880–1956) *In Defence of Women*,
> 1922, 'The Feminine Mind'.

41.   All men, except the most brutish, desire to have, in the
      woman most nearly connected with them, not a forced
      slave but a willing one.

> John Stuart Mill (1806–1873) *The Subjection of
> Women*, 1869, ch. 1.

42.   Whatever gratification of pride there is in the possession
      of power, and whatever personal interest in its exercise,
      is in this case [power over women] not confined to a
      limited class, but common to the whole male sex.

> John Stuart Mill (1806–1873) *ibid.*

43.   The legend of the jungle heritage and the evolution of

man as a hunting carnivore has taken root in man's mind . . . He may even believe that equal pay will do something terrible to his gonads.

> Elaine Morgan. *The Descent of Woman*, 1972, ch. 1.

44. To vigorous men intimacy is a matter of shame—and something precious.

> Friedrich Nietzsche (1844–1900) *Beyond Good and Evil*, 1885, ch. IV, 167.

45. There is a child hidden in the true man; and it wants to play. Come on then women, and find the child in man!

> Friedrich Nietzsche (1844–1900) *Thus Spake Zarathustra*, 1883–91, XVIII, 'Old and Young Women'.

46. Only he who is man enough will release the woman in woman.

> Friedrich Nietzsche (1844–1900) *ibid.* XLIX, 'The Belittling Virtue', 2.

47. Men are blind in their own cause.

> Proverb, 16th century.

48. Every man has his faults.

> Proverb, 16th century.

49. The bachelor is a peacock, the engaged man a lion, and the married man a jackass.

> German proverb.

50. What vain unnecessary things are men
How well we do without 'em, tell me then
Whence comes that mean submissiveness we find
This ill bred age has wrought on womankind.

> Earl of Rochester (1647–1680) *Satires*, LXII.

51. Never trust a husband too far, nor a bachelor too near.

> Helen Rowland (1876–1950) *The Rubaiyat of a Bachelor*, 1915.

52.   Men's vows are women's traitors.
>>> William Shakespeare (1564–1616) *Cymbeline*,
>>> 1610, III. iv.

53.   Men's evil manners live in brass; their virtues
We write in water.
>>> William Shakespeare (1564–1616) *Henry VIII*,
>>> 1612–13, IV. ii.

54.   Men's faults do seldom to themselves appear;
Their own transgressions partially they smother.
>>> William Shakespeare (1564–1616) *The Rape of*
>>> *Lucrece*, 1593–94.

55.   An odd man lady? every man is odd.
>>> William Shakespeare (1564–1616) *Troilus and Cressida*,
>>> 1597–1602, IV. v.

56.   All men make faults.
>>> William Shakespeare (1564–1616) *Sonnets*, 1593–1600,
>>> no. XXXV.

57.   It may be that male fears and insecurities about the
protection of their power and indispensability are more
well-founded than is generally thought!
>>> Sue Sharpe, *Just Like a Girl*, 1976, ch. VII,
>>> 'The Chosen Sex'.

58.   Except during the nine months before he draws his first
breath, no man manages his affairs as well as a tree does.
>>> George Bernard Shaw (1856–1950) *Maxims for*
>>> *Revolutionists*, 1903.

59.   Do you know what a pessimist is?
A man who thinks everybody as nasty as himself, and
hates them for it.
>>> George Bernard Shaw (1856–1950) *An Unsocial*
>>> *Socialist*, 1884, ch. 5.

60. In marriage, a man becomes slack and selfish, and undergoes a fatty degeneration of his moral being.
     Robert Louis Stevenson (1850–1894) *Virginibus Puerisque*, 1881, I.

61. Hunger and love are the two primitive motives behind men's actions—the two fundamental needs.
     Marie Carmichael Stopes (1880–1958) *Marriage in My Time*, 1935, ch. V.

62. A nice man is a man of nasty ideas.
     Jonathan Swift (1667–1745) *Thoughts on Various Subjects*, 1711.

63. The latter part of a wise man's life is taken up in curing the follies, prejudices, and false opinions he had contracted in the former.
     Jonathan Swift (1667–1745) *ibid*.

64. There's nothing so insecure as an aggressive human male in his mid-twenties.
     Warren Tute, *The Admiral*, 1963, part 3, ch. 4.

65. What hogs men turn, Belinda, when they grow weary of women!
     Sir John Vanbrugh (1664–1726) *The Provok'd Wife*, 1698, III. iii.

66. Gentlemen do not throw wine at ladies. They pour it over them.
     Auberon Waugh, *Observer*, 'Sayings of the Week', 19 June 1983.

67. Of two evils choose the prettier.
     Carolyn Wells (1862–1942). Quoted in J. Cooper and T. Hartman, *Violets and Vinegar*.

68. Give a man a free hand and he'll run it all over you.
     Mae West (1892–1980). Quoted in J. Green, *A Dictionary of Contemporary Quotations*.

69. A hard man is good to find—but you'll mostly find him asleep.

Mae West (1892–1980) Attributed.

70. If a woman wants to hold a man, she has merely to appeal to what is worst in him. We make gods of men and they leave us. Others make brutes of them and they fawn and are faithful.

Oscar Wilde (1854–1900) *Lady Windermere's Fan*, 1892, act III.

71. All men are married women's property. That is the only true definition of what married women's property really is.

Oscar Wilde (1854–1900) *A Woman of No Importance*, 1893, act II.

72. All power inebriates weak man.

Mary Wollstonecraft (1759–1797) *A Vindication of the Rights of Woman*, 1892, ch. I.

73. Men who have wasted a great part of their lives with women, and with whom they have sought for pleasure with eager thirst, entertain the meanest opinion of the sex.

Mary Wollstonecraft (1759–1797) *ibid*. ch. XIII, sect. VI.

74. The history of men's opposition to women's emancipation is more interesting perhaps than the story of that emancipation itself.

Virginia Woolf (1882–1941) *A Room of One's Own*, 1929.

67. Men and Women

1. Women were formed to temper mankind, and soothe them into tenderness and compassion; not to set an

edge upon their minds, and blow up in them those passions which are too apt to rise of their own accord.

> Joseph Addison (1672–1719) *The Spectator*, no. 57,
> 5 May 1711.

2. To men belong law, justice, science, and philosophy, all that is disinterested, universal and rational. Women, on the other hand, introduce into everything favour, exception, and personal prejudice.

> Henri-Frédéric Amiel (1821–1881) *Journal*,
> 13 May 1869.

3. If men are always deceived on the subject of women, it is because they forget that men and women do not speak the same language.

> Henri-Frédéric Amiel (1821–1881) *ibid*.
> 26 December 1868.

4. The only way a man can be a man is if a woman is a woman.

> Anonymous. Quoted in E. Janeway, *Man's World,*
> *Woman's Place*.

5. The male is by nature superior, and the female inferior: the one rules and the other is ruled.

> Aristotle (384–322 BC) *Politics*, book I, ch. 5.

6. No man naturally can imagine any more compelling business for a woman than being interested in him.

> Mary Austin (1868–1934) *A Woman of Genius*, 1912,
> book IV, ch. VI.

7. Physically a man is a man for much longer than a woman is a woman.

> Honoré de Balzac (1799–1850) Attributed.

8.   Man creates, woman conserves, man composes, woman interprets, man generalises, woman particularises, . . . man thinks more than he feels, woman feels more than she thinks.

> Earl Barnes (1861–1935) *Woman in Modern Society*, 1912.

9.   Man's the oak, woman's the ivy.

> J. M. Barrie (1860–1937) *What Every Woman Knows*, 1908 act III.

10.   While man *has* a sex, woman *is* a sex.

> E. Belfort Bax (1854–1926) *The Fraud of Feminism*, 1913, ch. II.

11.   It is not that men exercise tyranny over women; for their own good, and in the providence of God, it is a little the other way.

> Hilaire Belloc (1870–1953). Quoted in Antonia Raeburn, *Militant Suffragettes*.

12.   The woman is the glory of the man. For the man is not of the woman; but the woman of the man. Neither was the man created for the woman; but the woman for the man.

> Bible, Authorized Version, 1 Corinthians, 11:7–9.

13.   It takes a brave man to face a brave woman.

> Pearl S. Buck, *To my Daughters, With Love*, 1967.

14.   The fair-sex are so conscious to themselves that they have nothing in them which can deserve entirely to engross the whole man, that they heartily despise one who, to use their own expression, is always hanging at their apron-strings.

> Eustace Budgell (1686–1737) *The Spectator*, no. 506, 10 October 1712.

15. For man, to man so oft unjust,
    Is always so to women.
    > Lord Byron (1788–1824) *Don Juan*,
    > canto II, 1819, st. cc.

16. Every man is to be had one way or another, and every
    woman almost any way.
    > Lord Chesterfield (1694–1773). Letter to his son,
    > 5 June 1750.

17. The man's desire is for the woman; but the woman's
    desire is rarely other than for the desire of the man.
    > Samuel Taylor Coleridge (1772–1834) *Table Talk*,
    > 23 July 1827.

18. Lady Mary Wortley Montagu observed, that in the
    whole course of her long and extensive travels, she had
    found but two sorts of people, *men* and *women*.
    > C. C. Colton (1780–1832) *Lacon*, 1820, vol. I, 91.

19. Man differs from woman in size, bodily strength,
    hairiness, etc., as well as in mind, in the same manner as
    do the two sexes of many mammals.
    > Charles Darwin (1809–1882) *The Descent of Man*,
    > 1871, part I, ch I.

20. Women should not be expected to write, or fight, or
    build, or compose scores; she does all by inspiring man
    to do all.
    > Ralph Waldo Emerson (1803–1882) *Journal*, 1841.

21. When a woman behaves like a man, why doesn't she
    behave like a nice man?
    > Dame Edith Evans (1888–1976). Quoted in J. Cooper
    > and T. Hartman, *Violets and Vinegar*.

22. Sure men were born to lie, and women to believe them!
    > John Gay (1685–1732) *The Beggar's Opera*,
    > 1728, II. xiii.

23. Words are women, deeds are men.
      George Herbert (1593–1633) *Jacula Prudentum*, 1651.

24. Man has his will—but woman has her way!
      Oliver Wendell Holmes (1809–1894) *The Autocrat of the Breakfast-Table*, 1858, ch. II.

25. She shows her face with dignity,
      He admires, he keeps his pride.
      She may lose her dignity,
      But who will say who lied?

                                                            Peter James.

26. The silliest woman can manage a clever man; but it needs a very clever woman to manage a fool.
      Rudyard Kipling (1865–1936) *Plain Tales from the Hills*, 1888, 'Three and—an Extra'.

27. The art of being a woman can never consist of being a bad imitation of a man.
      Olga Knopf, *The Art of Being a Woman*, 1932, part 3, ch. 3.

28. As unto the bow the cord is,
      So unto the man is woman,
      Though she bends him, she obeys him,
      Though she draws him, yet she follows,
      Useless each without the other!
      Henry Wadsworth Longfellow (1807–1882) *The Song of Hiawatha*, 1855, X, 'Hiawatha's Wooing'.

29. The usual result of a man's cohabitation with a woman, however sanctioned by society, is to make him a little more petty, a little meaner than he would otherwise have been.
      W. Somerset Maugham (1874–1966) *A Writer's Notebook*, 1896.

30. Male and female are just as bad as one another.
      Guy de Maupassant (1850–1893) *Paul's Mistress*.

31. We know of no culture that has said, articulately, that there is no difference between men and women except in the way they contribute to the creation of the next generation.

> Margaret Mead (1901–1978) *Male and Female*, 1948, part I, ch. 1.

32. Men are made to be managed, and women are born managers.

> George Meredith (1828–1909) *The Ordeal of Richard Feverel*, 1859, ch. 34.

33. It is only a man here and there who has any tolerable knowledge of the character even of the women of his own family.

> John Stuart Mill (1806–1873) *The Subjection of Women*, 1869, ch. 1.

34. Whence true authority in men: though both
     Not equal, as their sex not equal seemed;
     For contemplation he and valour formed,
     For softness she and sweet attractive grace,
     He for God only, she for God in him.

> John Milton (1608–1674) *Paradise Lost*, 1667, book IV, l.295.

35. Howe'er man rules in science and in art,
     The sphere of woman's glories is the heart.

> Thomas Moore (1779–1852) *Epilogue*, written for Lady Dacre's *Tragedy of Ina*.

36. The sexes will naturally desire to appear to each other such as each believes the other will best like . . . and each sex will wish to appear more or less rational as they perceive it will more or less recommend them to the other.

> Hannah More (1745–1833) *Strictures on the Modern System of Female Education*, 1799, ch. XV.

37. Was she a great actress? Yes, I think so. Of course women act all the time. It is easier to judge a man.
    Iris Murdoch, *The Sea, The Sea*, 1980, 'Prehistory'.

38. The true man wants two different things: danger and diversion. Therefore he wants woman, as she is the most dangerous plaything.
    Friedrich Nietzsche (1844–1900) *Thus Spake Zarathustra*, 1883–91, XVIII, 'Old and Young Women'.

39. Man shall be trained for war, and woman for the recreation of the warrior: all else is folly.
    Friedrich Nietzsche (1844–1900) *ibid*.

40. Man thinks woman profound—why? Because he can never fathom her depths. Woman is not even shallow.
    Friedrich Nietzsche (1844–1900) *The Twilight of the Idols*, 1888, 'Maxims and Missiles', 27.

41. Men, some to bus'ness, some to pleasure take;
    But ev'ry woman is at heart a rake:
    Men, some to quiet, some to public strife;
    But ev'ry lady would be Queen for life.
    Alexander Pope (1688–1744) *Epistles to Several Persons*, II, 'To a Lady', l.215.

42. What's fame with men, by custom of the nation,
    Is call'd in women only reputation.
    Alexander Pope (1688–1744) *To a Lady with the Temple of Fame*.

43. What a man 'does' defines his status, but whom she marries defines a woman's.
    Alice S. Rossi, 'Women in Science: Why So Few?' *Science*, 28 May 1965.

44. The only problem with women is men.
    Kathie Sarachild. Quoted in J. Green, *A Dictionary of Contemporary Quotations*.

45. Men are not troubled to hear a man dispraised, because they know, though he be naught, there's worth in others; but women are mightily troubled to hear any of them spoken against, as if the sex itself were guilty of some unworthiness.

John Selden (1584–1654) *Table-Talk*, 1689, CLIII, 'Women'.

46. They [men] are all but stomachs, and we all but food:
They eat us hungerly, and when they are full,
They belch us.

William Shakespeare (1564–1616) *Othello*, 1604–5, III. iv.

47. Men have marble, women waxen minds.

William Shakespeare (1564–1616) *The Rape of Lucrece*, 1593–94.

48. Women may fall, when there's no strength in men.

William Shakespeare (1564–1616) *Romeo and Juliet*, 1595–96, II. iii.

49. I had too often heard men speak of women as if they were mere personal conveniences to feel surprised that exactly the same view is held, only more fastidiously, by women.

George Bernard Shaw (1856–1950) *Getting Married*, 1908, Preface.

50. The slavery of women means the tyranny of women. No fascinating woman ever wants to emancipate her sex: her object is to gather power into the hands of Man, because she knows that she can govern him. She is no more jealous of his nominal supremacy than he himself is jealous of the strength and speed of his horse.

George Bernard Shaw (1856–1950). Letter to Clement Scott, January 1902.

51. Can man be free if woman be a slave.

Percy Bysshe Shelley (1792–1822) *The Revolt of Islam*, 1817, II. xliii.

52. If you wish the pick of men and women, take a good
     bachelor and a good wife.

>   Robert Louis Stevenson (1850–1894) *Virginibus*
>   *Puerisque*, 1881, I.

53. Woman is the lesser man, and all thy passions, match'd
     with mine,
     Are as moonlight unto sunlight, and as water unto wine.

>   Alfred, Lord Tennyson (1809–1892) *Locksley Hall*,
>   1842.

54. Man dreams of fame while woman wakes to love.

>   Alfred, Lord Tennyson (1809–1892) *Merlin*
>   *and Vivien.*

55. For men at most differ as Heaven and Earth,
     But women, worst and best, as Heaven and Hell.

>   Alfred, Lord Tennyson (1809–1892) *ibid.*

56. Man for the field and woman for the hearth:
     Man for the sword and for the needle she:
     Man with the head and woman with the heart:
     Man to command and woman to obey;
     All else confusion.

>   Alfred, Lord Tennyson (1809–1892) *The Princess*,
>   1847, part V.

57. Man is the hunter; woman is his game:
     The sleek and shining creatures of the chase,
     We hunt them for the beauty of their skins;
     They love us for it, and we ride them down.

>   Alfred, Lord Tennyson (1809–1892) *ibid.*

58. 'Tis strange what a man may do, and a woman yet think
     him an angel.

>   William Makepeace Thackeray (1811–1863) *The*
>   *History of Henry Esmond*, 1852, book I, ch. VII.

59. Let our weakness be what it will, mankind will still be weaker; and whilst there is a world, 'tis woman that will govern it.

Sir John Vanbrugh (1664–1726) *The Provok'd Wife*, 1698, III. iii.

60. A man who moralises in usually a hypocrite, and a woman who moralises is invariably plain.

Oscar Wilde (1854–1900) *Lady Windermere's Fan*, 1892, act III.

61. I like men who have a future and women who have a past.

Oscar Wilde (1854–1900) *The Picture of Dorian Gray*, 1891, ch. 15.

62. *Lord Illingworth*: What do you call a bad man?
Mrs Allonby: The sort of man who admires innocence.
Lord Illingworth: And a bad woman?
Mrs Allonby: Oh! the sort of woman a man never gets tired of.

Oscar Wilde (1854–1900) *A Woman of No Importance*, 1893, act I.

63. Women represent the triumph of matter over mind—just as men represent the triumph of mind over morals.

Oscar Wilde (1854–1900) *ibid.* act III.

64. Terrible though the fact is as an indictment of the male sex, when a woman knows all, there is invariably trouble ahead for some man.

P. G. Wodehouse (1881–1975) *The Girl on the Boat*, 1922, ch. 15.

65. The two sexes mutually corrupt and improve each other.

Mary Wollstonecraft (1759–1797) *A Vindication of The Rights of Woman*, 1792, ch. VIII.

66. I have already animadverted on the bad habits which females aquire when they are shut up together; and, I think, that the observation may fairly be extended to the other sex.

> Mary Wollstonecraft (1759–1797) *ibid.* ch. XII.

67. From the tyranny of man, I firmly believe, the greater number of female follies proceed.

> Mary Wollstonecraft (1759–1797) *ibid.*
> ch. XIII, sect. VI.

68. Wherever one looked, men thought about women and thought differently.

> Virginia Woolf (1882–1941) *A Room of One's
> Own* 1929.

69. It would be a thousand pities if women wrote like men, or lived like men or looked like men.

> Virginia Woolf (1882–1941) *ibid.*

68. Mistresses

1. My advice is to keep two mistresses.
   Few men have the stamina for more.

> Ovid (43 BC–AD 17) *The Cures for Love,* AD 1.

2. I've always found it much more dangerous to fool with a man's mistress than his wife.

> Harold Robbins, *The Inheritors,* 1969, book 3, ch. 7.

3. No man has half that pleasure is possessing a mistress, as a woman has in jilting a gallant.

> Sir John Vanbrugh (1664–1726) *The Provok'd Wife,*
> 1698, I. i.

4. Next to the pleasure of making a new mistress is that of being rid of an old one.

> William Wycherley (1640–1716) *The Country Wife,*
> 1675, I. i.

5. A mistress should be like a little country retreat near the town—not to dwell in constantly, but only for a night and away, to taste the town the better.
> William Wycherley (1640–1716) *ibid*.

69. Modesty

1. Certainly most women magnify their modesty, for the same reason that cowards boast their courage, because they have least on't.
> George Farquhar (1678–1707) *The Constant Couple*, 1700, III. iii.

2. Women commend a modest man, but like him not.
> Thomas Fuller (1654–1734) *Gnomologia*, 1732.

3. Modesty—is a quality in a lover more praised by the women than liked.
> Richard Brinsley Sheridan (1751–1816) *The Rivals*, 1775, II. ii.

4. There is not upon earth so impertinent a thing as women's modesty.
> Sir John Vanbrugh (1664–1726) *The Provok'd Wife*, 1698, III. iii.

70. Money

(*See also* Wealth)

1. Cinderella married for money.
> Anonymous.

2. There's nothing turns men against a woman so much as to have her always thinking about money.
> Mary Austin (1868–1934) *A Woman of Genius*, 1912, book III, ch. IV.

3. There is only one thing for a man to do who is married to a woman who enjoys spending money, and that is to enjoy earning it.

> E. W. Howe, (1853–1937) *Country Town Sayings*, 1911.

4. A real woman has a special attitude toward money. If she earns it, it is hers; if her husband earns it, it is theirs.

> Joyce Jillson, *Real Women Don't Pump Gas*, 1982, ch. 6.

5. The wealthy woman who marries the money-loving husband might as well be unmarried.

> Juvenal (*c.* AD 60–*c.* 140) *Satires*, VI.

6. 'Mr Haley, she is not to be sold', said Shelby. 'My wife would not part with her for her weight in gold'.
'Ay, ay, women always say such things, 'cause they ha'nt no sort of calculation. Just show 'em how many watches, feathers, and trinkets one's weight in gold would buy, and that alters the case *I* reckon'.

> Harriet Beecher Stowe (1811–1896) *Uncle Tom's Cabin*, 1852, ch. 1.

71. Mothers

1. Mother's Day comes nine months after Father's Day.

> Anonymous.

2. Never marry a man who hates his mother because he'll end up hating you.

> Jill Bennett, *Observer*, 'Sayings of the Week', 12 September 1982.

3. She was maintaining the prime truth of woman, the universal mother: that if a thing is worth doing, it is worth doing badly.

> G. K. Chesterton (1874–1936) *What's Wrong with the World*, 1910, part IV, ch. 14.

4. The relationships between mothers and daughters are unfathomable, even for a psychologist of note. Men compete with their sons, but mothers devour their daughters.

    Len Deighton, *Goodbye Mickey Mouse*, 1982, ch. 13.

5. Men are what their mothers made them.

    Ralph Waldo Emerson (1803–1882) *The Conduct of Life*, 1860, 'Fate'.

6. In most societies woman is a paradox. She is dangerous, mysterious and an unclean thing but also, as a mother, the most revered.

    Sheila Kitzinger, *Women as Mothers*, 1978, ch. 10.

7. There is another mistake I forgot to mention usual in mothers. If any of their daughters are beauties, they take great pains to persuade them that they are ugly.

    Lady Mary Wortley Montagu (1689–1762). Letter to Lady Bute, 19 February 1750.

8. Motherhood is the most emotional experience of one's life. One joins a kind of women's mafia.

    Janet Suzman, *Observer*, 'Sayings of the Week', 19 July 1981.

9. No man is responsible for his father. That is entirely his mother's affair.

    Margaret Turnbull (?–1942) *Alabaster Lamps*, 1925.

10. There's a part of every man which resents the great big bossy woman that once made him eat up his spinach and wash behind his ears.

    Katherine Whitehorn, *Observer*, 16 January 1983.

11. *Lord Illingworth*: People's mothers always bore me to death. All women become like their mothers. That is their tragedy.
Mrs Allonby: No man does. That is his.
Oscar Wilde (1854–1900) *A Woman of No Importance*, 1893, act II.

12. The neglected wife is, in general, the best mother.
Mary Wollstonecraft (1759–1797) *A Vindication of the Rights of Woman*, 1792, ch. II.

13. The weakness of the mother will be visited on the children.
Mary Wollstonecraft (1759–1797) *ibid*. ch. XII.

72. Mothers-in-Law

1. Husbands with any pretensions at all to a knowledge of the science of marriage know that all they have to do is to confront their own mother with their wife's and they will be found to neutralise one another.
Honoré de Balzac (1799–1850) *The Physiology of Marriage*, 1829, part III, ch. XXV.

2. A wife should never be allowed to go alone to see her mother.
Honoré de Balzac (1799–1850) *ibid*.

3. The mother-in-law remembers not that she was a daughter-in-law.
Thomas Fuller (1654–1734) *Gnomologia*, 1732.

4. But there, everything has its drawbacks, as the man said when his mother-in-law died, and they came down on him for the funeral expenses.
Jerome K. Jerome (1859–1927) *Three Men in a Boat*, 1889, ch. 3.

5. While your mother-in-law is alive, domestic peace is out of the question.

> Juvenal (*c.* AD 60–*c.* 140) *Satires*, VI.

73. Obedience

1. The courage of a man is shown in commanding, of a woman in obeying.

> Aristotle (384–322 BC) *Politics*, book I, ch. 13.

2. She commandeth her husband in any equal matter by constantly obeying him.

> Thomas Fuller (1608–1661) *The Holy and the Profane State*, 1642, 'The Good Wife'.

3. Woman in her greatest perfection was made to serve and obey man, not to rule and command him.

> John Knox (1505–1572) *The First Blast of the Trumpet against the Monstrous Regiment of Women*, 1558.

4. Let it be proved that [women] ought to obey man implicitly, and I shall immediately agree that it is woman's duty to cultivate a fondness for dress, in order to please, and a propensity to cunning for her own preservation.

> Mary Wollstonecraft (1759–1797) *A Vindication of the Rights of Woman*, 1792, ch. XIII, sect. III.

74. Politics

1. Queens are better than kings, because under kings women govern, but under queens, men.

> Anonymous.

2. What difference does it make whether women rule, or the rulers are ruled by women? The result is the same.

> Aristotle (384–322 BC) *Politics*, book II, ch. 9.

3. All we men had grown used to our wives and mothers, and grandmothers, and great-aunts all pouring a chorus of contempt upon our hobbies of sport, drink and party politics. And now comes Miss Pankhurst, with tears in her eyes, owning that all the women were wrong and all the men were right.
    G. K. Chesterton (1874–1936) *What's Wrong with the World*, 1910, part III, ch. 7.

4. No sooner had women attained political equality, than they joined the men's parties, walking in the yoke of party discipline as submissively as they had been accustomed to doing under the guardianship of the men.
    Rosa Mayreder. Quoted in Marie Louise Janssen-Jarreit, *Sexism*.

5. Women are supposed to have no political power; but clever women put stupid husbands into parliament and into ministerial offices quite easily.
    George Bernard Shaw (1856–1950). Letter to Clement Scott, January 1902.

6. *Napoleon*: I can't stand women meddling in politics.
    Madame de Staël: Sire, in a country where women have been sent to the guillotine you can't blame them for asking why this happens to them.
    Mme. de Staël (1766–1817). Quoted in E. Larsen, *Wit as a Weapon*.

7. Woman's moral ideals are personal and domestic, as distinguished from impersonal and public.
    Sir Almroth E. Wright (1861–1947) *The Unexpurgated Case Against Woman Suffrage*, 1913, part II.

75. Polygamy

(*See also* Bigamy)

1. Hogamus higamus,
   Men are polygamous,
   Higamus hogamus,
   Women monogamous.

   Anonymous.

2. Polygamy, *n*. A house of atonement, or expiatory
   chapel, fitted with several stools of repentance, as
   distinguished from monogamy, which has but one.
   Ambrose Bierce (1842–*c*. 1914) *The Devil's
   Dictionary*, 1911.

3. Polygamy may well be held in dread,
   Not only as a sin, but as a *bore*:
   Most wise men with *one* moderate woman wed,
   Will scarcely find philosophy for more.
   Lord Byron (1788–1824) *Don Juan*,
   canto VI, 1823, st. xii.

76. Pornography

1. Pornography is the undiluted essence of anti-female
   propaganda.
   Susan Brownmiller, *Against Our Will*, 1975, ch. 12.

2. It'll be a sad day for sexual liberation when the
   pornography addict has to settle for the real thing.
   Brendan Francis. Quoted in E. F. Murphy, *The
   Macmillan Treasury of Relevant Quotations*.

111

77. Prostitution

1. Prostitution gives her an opportunity to meet people. It provides fresh air and wholesome exercise, and it keeps her out of trouble.

   Joseph Heller, *Catch—22*, 1975, ch. 33.

2. A man will not, once in a hundred instances, leave his wife and go to a harlot, if his wife has not been negligent of pleasing.

   Samuel Johnson (1709–1784) *Boswell's Life*, Spring 1768.

3. Prostitutes are a necessity. Without them men would attack respectable women in the streets.

   Napoleon I (1769–1821). Quoted in H. L. Mencken, *Dictionary of Quotations*.

4. It is a silly question to ask a prostitute why she does it . . . These are the highest paid 'professional' women in America.

   Gail Sheehy, *Hustling*, ch. 4.

5. Prostitutes believe in marriage. It provides them with most of their trade.

   'Suzie', *Knave*, 1975, vol. 7, no. 10.

78. Psychology/Psychiatry

1. The great question that has never been answered, and which I have not yet been able to answer despite my thirty years of research into the feminine soul is: What does a woman want?

   Sigmund Freud (1856–1939) Attributed

2. Penis envy is a myth. One reason to think so is that it bears the marks of originating on the male, not the female, side.

> Elizabeth Janeway, *Man's World, Woman's Place*, 1971, ch. 19.

3. An inherited collective image of woman exists in a man's unconsciousness, with the help of which he apprehends the nature of woman.

> C. G. Jung (1875–1961) *The Relations between the Ego and the Unconscious*, part 2, II.

4. Like a baboon's penis, [sports cars] stick out in front, they are long, smooth and shiny, they thrust forward with great vigour and they are frequently bright red in colour. A man sitting in his open sports car is like a piece of highly stylized phallic sculpture. His body has disappeared and all that can be seen are a tiny head and hands surmounting a long glistening penis.

> Desmond Morris, *The Human Zoo*, 1969, ch. 3.

5. A psychiatrist is a man who goes to the *Folies Bergère* and looks at the audience.

> Mervyn Stockwood. Attributed.

79. Rape

1. [Rape] is nothing more or less than a conscious process of intimidation by which *all men* keep *all women* in a state of fear.

> Susan Brownmiller, *Against our Will*, 1975, ch. 1.

2. Rather than society's aberrants or 'spoilers of purity', men who commit rape have served in effect as front-line masculine shock troops, terrorist guerrillas in the longest sustained battle the world has ever known.

> Susan Brownmiller, *ibid.* ch. 6.

3. All men are rapists and that's all they are. They rape us with their eyes, their laws and their codes.

> Marilyn French. Attributed.

4. It would be much better if young women should stop being raped much earlier in the proceedings than some of them do.

> Mr Justice Stabler, *Observer*, 'Sayings of the Week',
> 8 January 1961.

80. Religion

1. Even Mr Farley, the banker, who read books on evolution and was a Freethinker (opprobrious term), had been known to pronounce the church an excellent thing for women.

> Mary Austin (1868–1934) *A Woman of Genius*, 1912.
> book I, ch. VI.

2. It has been said that all sensible men are of the same religion and that no sensible man ever says what that religion is. So all sensible men are of the same opinion about women and no sensible man ever says what that opinion is.

> Samuel Butler (1835–1902) *Notebooks*, 1912,
> 'Higgledy-Piggledy'.

3. Men will wrangle for religion; write for it; fight for it; die for it; any thing but—*live* for it.

> C. C. Colton (1780–1832) *Lacon*, 1820, vol. I, 25.

4. The voice of God is the voice of man.

> Eva Figes, *Patriarchal Attitudes*, 1970, ch. 2.

5. Women are twice as religious as men; all the world knows that.

> Oliver Wendell Holmes (1809–1894) *The Professor at
> the Breakfast-Table*, 1860, ch. IX.

6. He for God only, she for God in him.
> John Milton (1608–1674) *Paradise Lost*, 1667,
> book IV, l.299 (*see also* 67.34).

7. Why Should We Not Pray to Our Mother Who Art in Heaven, As Well As to Our Father
> Elizabeth Cady Stanton (1815–1902) Headline in *The Revolution*, 30 July 1868.

81. Revenge

1. Since women do most delight in revenge, it may seem but feminine manhood to be vindictive.
> Sir Thomas Browne (1605–1682) *Christian Morals*,
> 1716, part III, sect. XII.

2. Sweet is revenge—especially to women.
> Lord Byron (1788–1824) *Don Juan*, canto I. 1819, st.
> cxxiv.

3. It is the weak petty mind that has pleasure in paying off scores, which is why no one enjoys revenge like a woman.
> Juvenal (*c.* AD 60–*c.* 140) *Satires*, XIII.

4. In revenge and in love woman is more barbarous than the man.
> Friedrich Nietzsche (1844–1900) *Beyond Good and Evil*, 1885, ch. IV, 139.

82. Secretaries

1. The corporation man sometimes emerges as much less than heroic to the one person in a real position to know—his secretary, on whom he often becomes markedly dependent.
> Myron Brenton, *The American Male*.

2. Different secretaries go different ways: some get laid and married, others old and harried.

    Arthur Hailey, *In High Places*, 1962, ch. 4.

83. Secrets

1. She is so very a woman, that she'll like thee the better for giving her the pleasure of telling a secret.

    Joseph Addison (1672–1719) *The Drummer*, 1716, II. i.

2. The most difficult secret for a man to keep is the opinion he has of himself.

    Anonymous.

3. I believe a woman only obliges a man to secrecy, that she may have the pleasure of telling herself.

    William Congreve (1670–1729) *Love for Love*, 1695, I. ii.

4. *Valentine*: I loved a woman, and loved her so long, that I found out a strange thing. I found out what a woman was good for.
    Tattle: Ay, prithee, what's that?
    Valentine: Why, to keep a secret.
    Tattle: O Lord!
    Valentine: O, exceeding good to keep a secret: for though she should tell, yet she is not to be believed.

    William Congreve (1670–1729) *ibid*. IV. iii.

5. He only is secret who never was trusted.

    Proverb.

6. The only secret a woman can keep is her age.

    Proverb.

7. The only secret a woman can keep is the one she doesn't know.

    French proverb.

8. No man should have a secret from his own wife. She invariably finds it out. Women have a wonderful instinct about things. They can discover everything except the obvious.

Oscar Wilde (1854–1900) *An Ideal Husband*, 1899, act II.

84. Seduction

1. And if a man entice a maid that is not betrothed, and lie with her, he shall surely endow her to be his wife.

Bible, Authorized Version, Exodus, 22:16.

2. 'Tis woman that seduces all mankind
By her we first were taught the wheedling arts.

John Gay (1685–1732) *The Beggar's Opera*, 1728, act I.

3.   What they [girls] love to yield
They would often rather have stolen. Rough seduction
Delights them, the boldness of near rape
Is a compliment

Ovid (43 BC–AD 17) *The Art of Love*, book I.

4. When a man seduces a woman, it should, I think, be termed a *left-handed* marriage.

Mary Wollstonecraft (1759–1797) *A Vindication of the Rights of Woman*, 1792, ch. IV.

85. Sex

1. If a lady says no she means may be, if she says may be she means yes, and if she says yes she's no lady.

Anonymous.

2. Being a sex symbol is a heavy load to carry, especially when one is tired, hurt and bewildered.

Clara Bow. Quoted in L. Halliwell, *The Filmgoer's Book of Quotes*.

3.   Men always fall for frigid women because they put on the best show.

> Fanny Brice (1891–1951). Quoted in L. J. Peter,
> *Peter's Quotations.*

4.   Let no woman believe a man's vows and wheedling talk, because when men are in a lustful mood, they are free with generous promises, which are forgotton as soon as they are satisfied.

> Catulus (87–*c.* 54 BC) *Poems*, LXIV.

5.   However much men say sex is not on their minds all the time, it is most of the time.

> Jackie Collins, *Observer*, 'Sayings of the Week',
> 19 July 1981.

6.   The big difference between sex for money and sex for free is that sex for money usually costs a lot less.

> Brendan Francis. Attributed.

7.   The rule in the women's colleges was that, after 7 pm, all men are beasts. Up until 7 pm they were all angels, and the girls simply had to learn to live with that routine and practice love in the afternoon.

> Harry G. Johnson (1923–1977) 'Cambridge in the
> 1950s', *Encounter*, January, 1974, p.30.

8.   Sex appeal is fifty per cent what you've got and fifty per cent what other people think you've got.

> Sophia Loren. Quoted in L. Halliwell, *The Filmgoer's
> Book of Quotes.*

9.   There is nothing about which men lie so much as their sexual powers. In this at least every man is, what in his heart he would like to be, a Casanova.

> W. Somerset Maugham (1874–1966) *A Writer's
> Notebook*, 1941.

10. A sex symbol becomes a thing. I hate being a thing.
> Marilyn Monroe (1926–1962). Quoted in L. Halliwell, *The Filmgoer's Book of Quotes*.

11. It takes two to make a woman into a sex object.
> Elaine Morgan, *The Descent of Woman*, 1972, ch. 12.

12. Marriage is for women the commonest mode of livelihood, and the total amount of undesired sex endured by women is probably greater in marriage than in prostitution.
> Bertrand Russell (1872–1970) *Marriage and Morals*, 1929, ch. XI.

13. Sexually, woman is nature's contrivance for perpetuating its highest achievement. Sexually, man is woman's contrivance for fulfilling nature's behest in the most economical way.
> George Bernard Shaw (1856–1950) *Man and Superman*, 1903, act III.

14. The way of women—when you will, they won't:
And when you won't, they're dying for you.
> Terence (190–159 BC) *The Eunuch*, IV. viii.

15. Female violence has increased by 192% in ten years. Other women, of course, have joined the League Against Cruel Sports or become lesbians and gone to Greenham Common. This is the sort of thing you must expect when you stop treating them as sex objects.
> Auberon Waugh, *Private Eye*, no. 557, 22 April 1983.

86. Sexism

(*See also* Feminism)

1. A general fling at the sex we may deem pardonable, for doing as little harm to womankind as the stone of an

119

urchin cast upon the bosom of mother earth; though men must look some day to have it returned to them.

> George Meredith (1828–1909) *Diana of the Crossways,*
> 1885, ch. I.

2. It is much more easy to accuse one sex than to excuse the other.

> Michel de Montaigne (1533–1592) *Essays,* 1595,
> book III, ch. V.

3. She lov'd to load mankind with blame,
   And on their errors build her fame.

> Hannah More (1745–1833) *The Lady and the Pye.*

4. Sexism isn't what it used to be.

> R. H. Parker. Attributed.

5. Peace will come when surplus of women shall have been removed by emigration.

> Sir Almroth E. Wright (1861–1947) *The
> Unexpurgated Case Against Woman
> Suffrage,* 1913, appendix.

87. Silence

1. A married man can be expected to yawn now and again—it is the only time he is allowed to open his mouth.

> Anonymous.

2. Women like quiet men: they think it means they are listening.

> Anonymous.

3. I have but one simile, and that's a blunder,
   For wordless women, which is *silent* thunder.

> Lord Byron (1788–1824) *Don Juan,*
> canto VI, 1823, st. lvii.

4. Women should be obscene and not heard.
> John Lennon (1941–1980). Quoted in J. Green, *A
> Dictionary of Contemporary Quotations*.

5. The silent man is the best to listen to.
> Japanese proverb.

6. A modest silence is a woman's crown.
> Sophocles (*c.* 496–406 BC). Quoted by Aristotle,
> *Politics*.

88. Sisters

1. Old maids never like and never have liked their sisters-in-law—that is the rule.
> Anton Chekhov (1860–1904) *The Three Sisters*,
> 1901, act III.

2. The brother had rather see his sister rich than make her so.
> Thomas Fuller (1654–1732) *Gnomologia*, 1732.

3. Never praise a sister to a sister, in the hope of your compliments reaching the proper ears ... Sisters are women first, and sisters afterwards.
> Rudyard Kipling (1865–1936) *Plain Tales from the
> Hills*, 1888, 'False Dawn'.

89. Social Class

1. It is women who, like mountain flowers, mark with most characteristic precision the graduation of social zones. The hierarchy of classes is clearly visible among them: it is blurred in the other sex.
> Henri-Frédéric Amiel (1821–1881) *Journal*,
> 6 May 1852.

2.   There's no social differences—till women come in.
     H. G. Wells (1866–1946) *Kipps*, 1905, book II, ch. IV.

90. Success

1.   Errors are notoriously hard to kill, but an error that
     ascribes to a man what was actually the work of a
     woman has more lives than a cat.
     [Referring to the assertion that Pierre and not Marie
     Curie discovered radium]
     Hertha Ayrton (1854–1923) *Westminster
     Gazette*, 14 March 1909.

2.   Many a man owes his success to his first wife, and his
     second wife to his success.
     Jim Backus. Quoted in J. Green, *A Dictionary of
     Contemporary Quotations.*

3.   A man is seldom ashamed of feeling that he cannot love
     a woman so well when he sees a certain greatness in her:
     nature having intended greatness for men.
     George Eliot (1819–1880) *Middlemarch*,
     1871, book IV, ch. 39.

4.   Progress in the Foreign Service is either vaginal or
     rectal. You marry the boss's daughter or you crawl up
     his bottom.
     Nicholas Monsarrat (1910–1979) *Smith and Jones*,
     1963, ch. 5.

5.   I sought for great men, but all I found were the apes of
     their ideal.
     Friedrich Nietzsche (1844–1900) *The Twilight of the
     Idols*, 1888, 'Maxims and Missiles', 39.

6.   There's only one way to get on for a woman, and that is
     to please men. That is what they think we are for.
     H. G. Wells (1866–1946) *Ann Veronica*, 1909, ch. II.

7. She's the kind of girl who climbed the ladder of success,
    wrong by wrong.
    > Mae West (1892–1980) *I'm No Angel*, 1933.

8. If we revert to history, we shall find that the women
    who have distinguished themselves have neither been
    the most distinguished nor the most gentle of their sex.
    > Mary Wollstonecraft (1759–1797) *A Vindication of the*
    > *Rights of Woman*, 1792, ch. II.

91. Talk

(*See also* The Tongue)

1. It has been said in the praise of some men, that they
    could talk whole hours together upon anything; but it
    must be owned to the honour of the other sex, that
    there are many among them who can talk whole hours
    together upon nothing.
    > Joseph Addison (1672–1791) *The Spectator*, no. 247,
    > 13 December 1711.

2. A question put in a Surrey school exam went 'Why do
    cocks crow early every morning?' A 12-year-old
    replied: 'My dad says they have to make the most of it
    while the hens are still asleep.'
    > Anonymous. Quoted by Peterborough, *Daily*
    > *Telegraph*, 9 March 1983.

3. Whether from shyness or precaution or artifice, a
    woman never speaks out her whole thought, and
    moreover what she herself knows of it is but a part of
    what it really is.
    > Henri-Frédéric Amiel (1821–1881) *Journal*, 26
    > December 1868.

4. For talk six times with the same single lady,
    And you may get the wedding-dresses ready.
    > Lord Byron (1788–1824) *Don Juan*, canto XII, 1823,
    > st. lix.

123

5. You are a woman, you must never speak what you think: your words must contradict your thoughts; but your actions may contradict your words.

> William Congreve (1670–1729) *Love for Love*,
> 1695, II. ii.

6. A woman without prattle, is like burgundy without spirit.

> Hannah Cowley (1743–1809) *A Bold Stroke for a*
> *Husband*, 1784, I. i.

7. Essentially feminine, she was able to chatter but say nothing, ask questions and require no reply.

> Len Deighton, *Goodbye Mickey Mouse*, 1982, ch. 12.

8. Talk to a man about himself and he will listen for hours.

> Benjamin Disraeli (1804–1881). Quoted in B. House,
> *From Eve On*.

9. Half the sorrows of women would be averted if they could repress the speech they know to be useless—nay, the speech they have resolved not to utter.

> George Eliot (1819–1880) *Felix Holt*, 1866, ch. 2.

10. Blessed is the man who, having nothing to say, abstains from giving wordy evidence of the fact.

> George Eliot (1819–1880) *The Impressions of*
> *Theophrastus Such*, 1879, ch. 4.

11. Much poor talk concerning woman, which at least had the effect of revealing the true sex of several of the party who usually go disguised in the form of the other sex.

> Ralph Waldo Emerson (1803–1882) *Journal*, 1843.

12. Men have always detested women's gossip because they suspect the truth: their measurements are being taken and compared.

> Erica Jong, *Fear of Flying*, 1974, ch. 5.

13. What women will say to other women, grumbling in their kitchens and complaining and gossiping, or what they make clear in their masochism, is often the last thing they will say aloud—a man may overhear.

> Doris Lessing, *The Golden Notebook*, 1962, preface.

14. There are no feminine characteristics more marked than a passion for detail and an unerring memory. Women can give you an exact and circumstantial account of some quite insignificant conversation with a friend years before; and what is worse, they do.

> W. Somerset Maugham (1874–1966) *A Writer's Notebook*, 1896.

15. It is only the very young girl at her first dinner-party whom it is difficult to entertain. At her second dinner-party, and thereafter, she knows the whole art of being amusing. All she has to do is listen; all we men have to do is to tell her about ourselves.

> A. A. Milne (1882–1956) *If I May*, 1920.

16. Concerning women, one should only talk to men.

> Friedrich Nietzsche (1844–1900) *Thus Spake Zarathustra*, 1883–91, XVIII, 'Old and Young Women'.

17. The only remedy against this interminable talking of the wife was the deafness of the husband.

> François Rabelais (*c.* 1494–1553) *Pantagruel*, 1532, book III, ch. XXXIV.

18. Man says what he knows, woman what she pleases.

> Jean-Jacques Rousseau (1712–1778) *Émile*, 1762, book V, part I.

19. Do you not know I am a woman? When I think, I must speak.

> William Shakespeare (1564–1616) *As You Like It*, 1596–1600, III. ii.

20. To be slow in words is a woman's only virtue.
    William Shakespeare (1564–1616) *Two Gentlemen of Verona*, 1594–95, III. i.

21. A healthy male bore consumes *each year* one and a half times his own weight in other people's patience.
    John Updike, *Assorted Prose*, 1965, 'Confessions of a Wild Bore'.

22. But the true male never yet walked
    Who liked to listen when his mate talked.
    Anna Wickham (1884–1947) *The Affinity*.

92. Temper

1. The spleen, madam, is a female frailty that I have no pretentions to, nor any of its affections.
   John Gay (1685–1732) *Achilles*, 1733, act I.

2. The first and most important attribute to a woman is good temper: formed to obey so imperfect a being as man.
   Jean-Jacques Rousseau (1712–1778) *Émile*, 1762, book V, part I.

3. Nothing is so aggravating as calmness. There is something positively brutal about the good temper of most modern men. I wonder we women stand it as well as we do.
   Oscar Wilde (1854–1900) *A Woman of No Importance*, 1893, act II.

93. The Tongue

(*See also* Talk)

1. I have often been puzzled to assign a cause why women should have this talent of ready utterance in so much

greater perfection than men. I have sometimes fancied that they have not a retentive power, or the faculty of suppressing their thoughts, as men have, but that they are necessitated to speak every thing they think and if so, it would perhaps furnish a very strong argument to the Cartesians . . . supporting . . . their doctrine that the soul always thinks. But as several are of the opinion that the fair-sex are not altogether strangers to the art of dissembling and concealing their thoughts, I have been forced to relinquish that opinion, and have therefore endeavoured to seek after some better reason. In order to do it a friend of mine, who is an excellent anatomist, has promised me by the first opportunity to dissect a woman's tongue, and to examine whether there may not be in it certain juices which render it so wonderfully voluble or flippant, or whether the fibres of it may not be made up of a finer or more pliant thread; or whether there are not in it some particular muscles which dart it up and down by such sudden glances and vibrations; or whether in the last place, there may not be certain undiscovered channels running from the head and the heart to this little instrument of loquacity, and conveying into it a perpetual affluency of animal spirits.

Joseph Addison (1672–1719) *The Spectator*, no. 247,
13 December 1711.

2.   Trust not a man with a too caressing tongue.

Cato (234–149 BC). Quoted in B. House,
From Eve On.

3.   When a man dies, the last thing that moves is his heart; in a woman her tongue.

George Chapman (*c*. 1559–1634) *The Widow's Tears*,
1612, IV. iii.

4.   Men are born with *two* eyes, but with *one* tongue, in order that they should see twice as much as they say; but, from their conduct, one would suppose that they were born with two tongues, and one eye, for those talk

127

the most who have observed the least, and obtrude their remarks upon everything, who have seen *into* nothing.

C. C. Colton (1780–1832) *Lacon*, 1820, vol. I, 112.

5. Tongue; well that's a wery good thing when it an't a woman's.

Charles Dickens·(1812–1870) *The Pickwick Papers*,
1837, ch. 19.

6. Though woman's glib tongue, when her passions are fir'd,
Eternally go, a man's ear can be tir'd
Since woman will have both her word and her way.

John Gay (1685–1732) *Achilles*, 1733, act I.

7. The tongue is a woman's weapon.

John Gay (1685–1732) *ibid.* act III.

8. An ox is taken by the horns, and a man by the tongue.

George Herbert (1593–1633) *Jacula Prudentum*, 1651.

9. Now the men were all like women
Only used their tongues for weapons!

Henry Wadsworth Longfellow (1807–1882) *The Song
of Hiawatha*, 1855, X, 'Hiawatha's Wooing'.

10. If you would make a good pair of shoes, take for the sole the tongue of a woman; it never wears out.

Proverb.

11. A fluent tongue is the only thing a mother don't like her daughter to resemble her in.

Richard Brinsley Sheridan (1751–1816) *St. Patrick's
Day*, 1775, I. ii.

94. Trust

1. You can never trust a woman: she may be true to you.

Douglas Ainslie (1865–1948) Attributed.

2. Woman hides her form from the eyes of men in our world: they cannot, she rightly thinks, be trusted.
    Ralph Waldo Emerson (1803–1882) *Journal*, 1841.

3. I wonder men dare trust themselves with men.
    William Shakespeare (1564–1616) *Timon of Athens*, 1607–8, I. ii.

4. Distrust that man who tells you to distrust.
    Ella Wheeler Wilcox (1855–1919) *Distrust*.

5. London is full of women who trust their husbands. One can always recognise them. They look so thoroughly unhappy.
    Oscar Wilde (1854–1900) *Lady Windermere's Fan*, 1892, act II.

95. Vanity

1. Men try to explain the feminine cult of clothes by asserting that women as a sex are vain. It is a profound truth that women as a sex are vain. It is also a profound truth that men as a sex are vain. Have you ever been with a man into a hosier's shop?
    Arnold Bennett (1867–1931) *Self and Self-Management*, 1911, 'The Meaning of Frocks'.

2. You will easily discover every man's prevailing vanity by observing his favourite topic of conversation.
    Lord Chesterfield (1694–1773). Letter to his son, 16 October 1747.

3. Carlos! I know your sex: the vainest female, in the hour of her exultation and power, is still out-done by man in vanity.
    Hannah Cowley (1743–1809) *A Bold Stroke for a Husband*, 1784, II. i.

129

4. Feminine vanity: that divine gift which makes women charming.
>   Benjamin Disraeli (1804–1881) *Tancred*, 1847,
>   book II, ch. VIII.

5. Every pretty woman studies her face, and a looking-glass to her is what a book is to a pedant; she is poring upon it all day long.
>   John Gay (1685–1732) *Polly*, 1729, act I.

6. Men's vanity will often dispose them to be commended into very troublesome employments.
>   Lord Halifax (1633–1695) *Moral Thoughts and
>   Reflections*, 1750.

7. The more women look in their glass, the less they look to their house.
>   George Herbert (1593–1633) *Jacula Prudentum*, 1651.

8. Very few pretty women can see anything, since vanity precludes glasses.
>   Iris Murdoch, *The Sea, The Sea*, 1980, 'Prehistory'.

9. In the background of all their personal vanity, women themselves have still their impersonal scorn—for 'woman'.
>   Friedrich Nietzsche (1844–1900) *Beyond Good and
>   Evil*, 1885, ch. IV, 86.

10. If ladies be but young and fair
     They have the gift to know it.
>   William Shakespeare (1564–1616) *As You Like It*,
>   1596–1600, II. vii.

11. For there was never yet fair woman but she made mouths in a glass.
>   William Shakespeare (1564–1616) *King Lear*,
>   1605–6, III. ii.

12. It is wonderful how far a fond opinion of herself can carry a woman.

> Sir Richard Steele (1672–1729) *The Spectator*, no. 156,
> 29 August 1711.

13. A man must endeavour to look wholesome, lest he makes so nauseous a figure in the side-box, the ladies should be compell'd to turn their eyes upon the play.

> Sir John Vanbrugh (1664–1726) *The Relapse*,
> 1697, II. i.

96. Virginity

1. Sire, four virgins wait without.
Without what?
Without food and clothing.
Give them food and bring them in.

> Anonymous. Quoted in K. Whitehorn,
> *Only on Sundays*.

2. If a virgin marry, she hath not sinned.

> *Bible*, Authorized Version, 1 Corinthians, 7:28.

3. Nature abhors a virgin—a frozen asset.

> Clare Boothe Luce. Quoted in L. & M. Cowan,
> *The Wit of Woman*.

4. No, no; for my virginity,
When I lose that, says Rose, I'll die:
Behind the elms last night, cried Dick,
Rose, were you not extremely sick?

> Matthew Prior (1664–1721) *A True Maid*.

5. Loss of virginity is rational increase; and there was never virgin got till virginity was first lost.

> William Shakespeare (1564–1616) *All's Well That
> Ends Well*, 1602–4, I. i.

6. Not for me the cold calm kiss
   Of a virgin's bloodless love.
   > Ella Wheeler Wilcox (1855–1919) *I Love You.*

97. Virtue

1. Ugliness, *n.* A gift of the gods to certain women, entailing virtue without humility.
   > Ambrose Bierce (1842–c. 1914) *The Devil's Dictionary*, 1911.

2. If one woman's virtue depended upon another's suspicions, where wou'd we find a woman of common modesty!
   > John Gay (1685–1732) *Achilles*, 1733, act I.

3. Most virtuous women are hidden treasures, who are not kept in safety because they are not searched for.
   > François, Duc de La Rochefoucauld (1613–1680) *Maxims*, 1678.

4. Woman's virtue is man's greatest invention.
   > Cornelia Otis Skinner (1901–1979) Attributed.

5. The man who had some virtue whilst he was struggling for a crown, often becomes a voluptuous tyrant when it graces his brow.
   > Mary Wollstonecraft (1759–1797) *A Vindication of the Rights of Woman*, 1792, ch. II.

6. It is vain to expect virtue from women till they are in the same degree independent of men; nay, it is vain to expect that strength of natural affection which would make them good wives and mothers. Whilst they are absolutely dependent on their husbands they will be cunning, mean, and selfish.
   > Mary Wollstonecraft (1759–1797) *ibid.* ch. IX.

7. Let woman share the rights, and she will emulate the virtues of man.
    Mary Wollstonecraft (1759–1797) *ibid.*
    ch. XIII, sect. VI.

98. Wealth

(*See also* Money)

1. All heiresses are beautiful.
    John Dryden (1631–1700) *King Arthur*, 1691, I. i.

2. No woman can be a beauty without a fortune.
    George Farquhar (1678–1707) *The Beaux Stratagem*,
    1707, II. ii.

3. His designs were strictly honourable, as the phrase is; that is, to rob a lady of her fortune by way of marriage.
    Henry Fielding (1707–1754) *Tom Jones*, 1749,
    book XI, ch. IV.

4. No rich man is ugly.
    Zsa Zsa Gabor. Quoted in *The Sunday Times*,
    26 October 1975.

5. A poor beauty finds more lovers than husbands.
    George Herbert (1593–1633) *Jacula Prudentum*, 1651.

6. Remember, it's as easy to marry a rich woman as a poor woman.
    William Makepeace Thackeray (1811–1863) *The
    History of Pendennis*, 1849, ch. XXVIII.

99. Weddings

1. It is a singular fact, worthy of study by the anthropologists, that a month or two before his daughter's marriage, the father, the husband, the bread

winner, who has made the whole affair possible, is afflicted with imbecility—that is, in the estimation of the female members of the tribe. They fuss and buzz about like a swarm of bees, arranging, planning, arguing, advising, whispering in corners, yelling over the telephone, buying this and ordering that. The only person never consulted, never allowed to open his mouth, is Daddy, who 'doesn't understand'.

> A. P. Herbert (1890–1971) *More Uncommon Law*,
> 1982, 'Who Giveth this Woman?'

2. A man may weep on his wedding day.

> William Shakespeare (1564–1616) *Henry VIII*,
> 1612–13, Prologue.

3. Marriage: a ceremony in which rings are put on the finger of the lady and through the nose of the gentleman.

> Herbert Spencer (1820–1903) Attributed.

100. Widowers

1. A married man can do anything he likes if his wife don't mind. A widower can't be too careful.

> George Bernard Shaw (1856–1950) *Misalliance*, 1910.

101. Widows

1. *Sir George Truman*: How long did her grief last?
    Vellum: Longer than I have know any widow's—at least three days.

> Joseph Addison (1672–1719) *The Drummer*,
> 1716, II. i.

2. I do not know yet how to deal with sufficient tenderness and without exasperation with the disposition of widowed women, bred to dependence, to build out of their sons the shape of a man proper to be leaned upon.

    Mary Austin (1868–1934) *A Woman of Genius*, 1912,
    book I, ch. VI.

3. Honour is, like a widow, won
    With brisk attempt and putting on;
    With entring manfully, and urging;
    Not slow approaches, like a virgin.

    Samuel Butler (1612–1680) *Hudibras*, 1663,
    part I, canto I, l.905.

4. Be wery careful o' widders all your life, specially if they've kept a public-house.

    Charles Dickens (1812–1870) *The Pickwick Papers*.
    1837, ch. 20.

5. When widows exclaim loudly against second marriages, I would always lay a wager that the man, if not the wedding day, is absolutely fixed on.

    Henry Fielding (1707–1754) *Amelia*, 1751,
    book VI, ch. VIII.

6. The comfortable estate of widowhood is the only hope that keeps up a wife's spirits.

    John Gay (1685–1732) *The Beggar's Opera*, 1728, I. x.

7. You must ev'n do like other widows; buy yourself weeds and be cheerful.

    John Gay (1685–1732) *ibid*. II. xii.

8. Her husband's funeral
    Is often where a widow looks for the next man.

    Ovid (43 BC–AD 17) *The Art of Love*, book III.

102. Wit

1. It has been said, that to excel them in wit, is a thing the men find is the most difficult to pardon in the women.
C C. Colton (1780–1832) *Lacon*, 1820, vol. I, 137.

2. A woman's wit
Lets daylight through you ere you know you're hit.
Oliver Wendell Holmes (1809–1894) *The Autocrat of the Breakfast-Table*, 1858, ch. II.

3. A very little wit is valued in a woman; as we are pleased with a few words spoken plain by a parrot.
Jonathan Swift (1667–1745) *Thoughts on Various Subjects*, 1711.

103. Wives

(*See also* Husbands and Wives)

1. Wives are young men's mistresses; companions for middle age; and old men's nurses.
Francis Bacon (1561–1626) *Essays*, 1597, VIII, 'Of Marriage and Single Life'.

2. Many husbands find it difficult to keep their wives from reading, and there are even some who contend that reading has this advantage, that at least they know what their wives are doing.
Honoré de Balzac (1799–1850) *The Physiology of Marriage*, 1829, part II, ch. XI.

3. Every man who is high up loves to think that he has done it all himself; and the wife smiles, and lets it go at that. It's our only joke. Every woman knows that.
J. M. Barrie (1860–1937) *What Every Woman Knows*, 1908, act IV.

4. Helpmate, *n.* A wife, or bitter half.
> Ambrose Bierce (1842–*c.* 1914) *Devil's Dictionary*, 1911.

5. Curs'd be the man, the poorest wretch in life,
The crouching vassal to the tyrant wife!
Who has no will but by her high permission;
Who has not sixpence but in her possession;
Who must to her his dear friend's secrets tell;
Who dreads a curtain-lecture worse than hell!
> Robert Burns (1759–1796) *On the Henpecked Husband.*

6. The elegant female, vapid and fading away to nothing still feels faintly the fundamental difference between herself and her husband; that he must be Something in the City, that she may be everything in the country.
> G. K. Chesterton (1874–1936) *What's Wrong with the World*, 1910, part IV, ch. 14.

7. A woman, let her be as good as she may, has got to put up with the life her husband makes for her.
> George Eliot (1819–1880) *Middlemarch*, 1871, book III, ch. 25.

8. In choosing a wife, and buying a sword, we ought not to trust another.
> George Herbert (1593–1633) *Jacula Prudentum*, 1651.

9. Who lets his wife go to every feast, and his horse drink at every water, shall neither have good wife nor good horse.
> George Herbert (1593–1633) *ibid.*

10. A good wife maketh a good husband.
> John Heywood (*c.* 1497–*c.* 1580) Proverbs, 1546.

11. A wife is not to be her husband's judge.
> Henrick Ibsen (1828–1906) *Ghosts*, 1881, act I.

12. Some cunning men choose fools for their wives, thinking to manage them, but they always fail.

Samuel Johnson (1709–1784) *The Tour to the Hebrides*, 19 September 1773.

13. Can no one find the art of gaining the love of his wife?

Jean de La Bruyère (1654–1696) *Characters*, 1688, 'Of Women', 80.

14. When a wife keeps her man under close lock and key
And herself goes wherever she will;
I think in this case everyone will agree
That Jack is the lady not Jill.

Martial (*c.* AD 40–*c.* 104) *Epigrams*, trans. Pott and Wright, book X, lxix.

15. You ask why I won't marry a rich wife? Because I don't want to pass as my wife's husband. The wife should be inferior to the husband. That is the only way to insure equality between the two.

Martial (*c.* AD 40–*c.* 104). Quoted in B. House, *From Eve On*

16. There is never any want of women who complain of ill-usage by their husbands.

John Stuart Mill (1806–1873) *The Subjection of Women*, 1869, ch. 1.

17. The wife's power of being disagreeable generally only establishes a counter-tyranny, and makes victims in their turn chiefly of those husbands who are least inclined to be tyrants.

John Stuart Mill (1806–1873) *ibid*. ch. II.

18. [A wife] pleases her husband when she doesn't please anyone else.

Molière (1622–1673) *The School for Wives*, 1662, III, ii, 4th maxim.

19.   The cloy of all pleasure, the luggage of life,
      Is the best that can be said for a very good wife.
                         Earl of Rochester (1647–1680) *On a Wife.*

20.   Married women are kept women, and they are
      beginning to find it out.
                         Logan Pearsall Smith (1865–1946)
                         Afterthoughts, 1931.

21.   God save us all from wives who are angels in the street,
      saints in the church and devils at home.
                         Charles Haddon Spurgeon (1834–1892) *John
                         Ploughman*, 1880, ch. 3.

22.   If I may speak, after profound and extensive study and
      observation, there are few better ways of securing the
      faithfulness and admiration of the beautiful partners of
      our existence than a little judicious ill treatment, a brisk
      dose of occasional violence as an alternative, and, for
      general and wholesome diet, a cooling but pretty
      constant neglect. At sparing intervals, administer small
      quantities of love and kindness; but not every day, or
      too often, as this medicine, much taken loses its effect.
      Those dear creatures who are most indifferent to their
      husbands, are those who are cloyed by too much
      surfeiting of the sugar plums and lollipops of love.
                         William Makepeace Thackeray (1811–1863) *The
                         Virginians*, 1857, vol. I, ch. 35.

23.   Auntie says, with manner grave,
      'Wife is synonym for slave'.
                         Ella Wheeler Wilcox (1855–1919) *To Marry or
                         Not to Marry?*

24.   He that shows his wife or money will be in danger of
      having them borrowed sometimes.
                         William Wycherley (1640–1716) *The Country Wife*,
                         1675, III. ii.

25. A man likes his wife to be just clever enough to comprehend his cleverness, and just stupid enough to admire it.

> Israel Zangwill (1864–1926) Attributed.

104. Women

1. The woman that deliberates is lost.

> Joseph Addison (1672–1719) *Cato*, 1721, IV. i.

2. I shou'd think myself a very bad woman if I had done what I do, for a farthing less.

> Joseph Addison (1672–1719) *The Drummer*, 1716, I. i.

3. It is hard to know what a woman believes.

> Joseph Addison (1672–1719) *ibid*. III. i.

4. There is not so great a difference between woman and woman, as you imagine.

> Joseph Addison (1672–1719) *ibid*. IV. i.

5. One of the fathers, if I am rightly informed, has defined a woman to be an animal that delights in finery. I have . . . observed, that in all ages they have been more careful than the men to adorn that part of the head which we generally call the outside.

> Joseph Addison (1672–1719) *The Spectator*, no. 265, 3 January 1712.

6. Anyone who sees through women is missing a lot.

> Anonymous.

7. He that possesses a woman's body possesses her soul.

> Anonymous.

8. No wild beast is there, no flame of fire, more fierce and untameable than woman; the panther is less savage and shameless.

> Aristophanes (*c.* 448–*c.* 388 BC) *Lysistrata*, 411 BC.

9. Oh! those confounded women! how they do cajole us! How true is the saying: "'Tis impossible to live with the baggages, impossible to live without them"!
   Aristophanes (*c.* 448–*c.* 388 BC) *ibid.*

10. There is but one thing in the world worse than a shameless woman, and that's another woman.
    Aristophanes (*c.* 448–*c.* 388 BC) *The Thesmophoriazusae*, 410 BC.

11. The life of a gifted woman is, in respect to the things that are supposed to count most with women, always a squalid affair.
    Mary Austin (1868–1934) *A Woman of Genius*, 1912, book IV, ch. I.

12. Most women are not thinking at all what they are very willing to be thought of as thinking.
    Mary Austin (1868–1934) *ibid.* ch. IX.

13. A sweetheart is a bottle of wine; a wife is a wine bottle.
    Charles Baudelaire (1821–1867). Quoted in B. House, *From Eve On*.

14. The dogma of women's complete historical subjection to men must be rated as one of the most fantastic myths ever created by the human mind.
    Mary Ritter Beard (1876–1958) *Women as a Force in History*, 1946.

15. There is no other purgatory but a woman.
    Francis Beaumont (1584–1616) and John Fletcher (1579–1625) *The Scornful Lady*, 1616, III. i.

16. One is not born, but rather becomes a woman.
    Simone de Beauvoir. *The Second Sex*, 1949, part IV, ch. 1.

17. Let the women learn in silence with all subjection. But I suffer not a woman to teach, not to usurp authority

over the man, but to be in silence. For Adam was first formed, then Eve. And Adam was not deceived, but the woman being deceived was in the transgression.

> *Bible*, Authorized Version, I Timothy, 2:11–15.

18. Indiscretion, *n*. The guilt of women.

> Ambrose Bierce (1842–*c*. 1914) *The Devil's Dictionary*, 1911.

19. Lap, *n*. One of the most important organs of the female system—an admirable provision of nature for the repose of infancy, but chiefly useful in rural festivities to support plates of cold chicken and heads of adult males.

> Ambrose Bierce (1842–*c*. 1914) *ibid*.

20. Woman, *n*. An animal usually living in the vicinity of Man, and having a rudimentary susceptibility to domestication.

> Ambrose Bierce (1842–*c*. 1914) *ibid*.

21. But there's wisdom in women, of more than they have known,
And thoughts go blowing through them, are wiser than their own.

> Rupert Brooke (1887–1915) *There's Wisdom in Women*, 1913.

22. A woman very much settles her esteem for a man, according to the figure he makes in the world, and the character he bears among his own sex.

> Eustace Budgell (1686–1737) *The Spectator*, no. 506, 10 October 1712.

23. Women, you know, do seldom fail,
To make the stoutest men turn tail.

> Samuel Butler (1612–80) *Hudibras*, 1663, part III, canto I, l.1,081.

24. What a strange thing is Man! and what a stranger
     Is Woman! What a whirlwind is her head,
     And what a whirlpool full of depth and danger
     Is all the rest about her!
>   Lord Byron (1788–1824) *Don Juan*, canto IX,
>   1823, st. lxiv.

25. I have always found women difficult.
>   Barbara Cartland, *The Isthmus Years*, ch. 8.

26. Truly woman's made of glass.
>   Miguel de Cervantes (1547–1616) *Don Quixote*,
>   1605–15, part I, ch. 33.

27. A lot of men, especially careless men like you and your
     employer, could go on saying for days that something
     ought to be done, or might as well be done. But if you
     convey to a woman that something ought to be done,
     there is always a dreadful danger that she will suddenly
     do it.
>   G. K. Chesterton (1874–1936) *The Secret of Father
>   Brown*, 1927, 'The Song of the Flying Fish'.

28. Every woman is a captive queen. But every crowd of
     women is only a harem broken loose.
>   G. K. Chesterton (1874–1936) *What's Wrong with the
>   World*, 1910, part III, ch. 4.

29. In all legends men have thought of women as sublime
     separately but horrible in a herd.
>   G. K. Chesterton (1874–1936) *ibid*. ch. 11.

30. Women, like flames, have a destroying power
     Ne'er to be quenched till they themselves devour.
>   William Congreve (1670–1729) *The Double-Dealer*,
>   1694, IV. v.

31. Women are like tricks by sleight of hand,
     Which, to admire, we should not understand.
>   William Congreve (1670–1729) *Love for Love*,
>   1695, IV. iii.

32.　Every woman is the same.
　　　　William Congreve (1670–1729) *The Old Bachelor*,
　　　　　　　　　　1693, II. ii.

33.　A woman, and ignorant, may be honest, when 'tis out
　　of obstinacy and contradiction; but, 'sdeath! it is but a
　　may-be, and upon scurvy terms.
　　　　William Congreve (1670–1729) *ibid*. III. iv.

34.　What is woman?—only one of nature's agreeable
　　blunders.
　　　　Hannah Cowley (1743–1809) *Who's the Dupe?*,
　　　　　　　　　　1779, II. ii.

35.　Woman's knowledge of man as part of her armoury for
　　survival is as old as Eve.
　　　　Maxine Davis. *The Sexual Responsibility of Woman*,
　　　　　　　　　　1957, ch. 1.

36.　　She knew treachery,
　　Rapine, deceit, and lust, and ills enow
　　To be a woman.
　　　　John Donne (*c*. 1571–1631) *Progress of the
　　　　　　　　　　Soul*, 1612, LI.

37.　There are only three things to be done with a woman.
　　You can love her, suffer for her, or turn her into
　　literature.
　　　　Lawrence Durrell, *Justine*, 1957.

38.　A woman's hopes are woven of sunbeams; a shadow
　　annihilates them.
　　　　George Eliot (1819–1880) *Felix Holt*, 1866, ch. I.

39.　How rarely can a female mind be impersonal.
　　　　Ralph Waldo Emerson (1803–1882) *Journal*, 1836.

40. Women are like pictures of no value in the hands of a fool, till he hears men of sense bid high for the purchase.

> George Farquhar (1678–1707) *The Beaux Stratagem*, 1707, II. i.

41. Why should I be angry that a woman is a woman? Since inconstancy and falsehood are grounded in their natures, how can they help it?

> George Farquhar (1678–1707) *The Constant Couple*, 1700, II. iii.

42. A woman who hath once been pleased with the possession of a man, will go above half way to the devil to prevent any other woman from enjoying the same.

> Henry Fielding (1707–1754) *Tom Jones*, 1749, book XVI, ch. IV.

43. Women are equal because they are not different any more.

> Erich Fromm, *The Art of Loving*, 1956.

44. I can see her faults, sir. I see her as a woman sees a woman.

> John Gay (1685–1732) *Achilles*, 1733, act I.

45. Of all the plagues with which the world is curst,
Of every ill, a woman is the worst.

> George Granville, Baron Lansdowne (1667–1735) *The British Enchanters*, 1706.

46. Women never reason, and therefore they are (comparatively) seldom wrong.

> William Hazlitt (1778–1830) *Characteristics*, 1832.

47. Women have no need to prove their manhood.

> Wilma Scott Heide. Quoted in Lisa Leghorn and Katherine Parker, *Sexual Economics and the World of Men*.

48. She plucked from my lapel the invisible strand of lint (the universal act of a woman to proclaim ownership).
      O. Henry (1862–1910) *Strictly Business*, 1910, 'A Ramble in Aphasia'.

49. Discreet women have neither eyes nor ears.
      George Herbert (1593–1633) *Jacula Prudentum*, 1651.

50. Women laugh when they can, and weep when they will.
      George Herbert (1593–1633) *ibid*.

51. Nature is in earnest when she makes a woman.
      Oliver Wendell Holmes (1809–1894) *The Autocrat of the Breakfast-Table*, 1858, ch. XII.

52. A woman never forgets her sex. She would rather talk with a man than an angel, any day.
      Oliver Wendell Holmes (1809–1894) *The Poet at the Breakfast-Table*, 1872, ch. IV.

53. A woman, notwithstanding she is the best of listeners, knows her business, and it is a woman's business to please.
      Oliver Wendell Holmes (1809–1894) *ibid*.

54. Womanly women are very kindly critics, except to themselves and now and then to their own sex. The less there is of sex about a woman, the more she is to be dreaded.
      Oliver Wendell Holmes (1809–1894) *ibid*.

55. Women are such strange creatures! Is there any trick that love and their own fancies do not play them? Just see how they marry!
      Oliver Wendell Holmes (1809–1894) *The Professor at the Breakfast-Table*, 1860, ch. VII.

56. But, alas! alas! for the woman's fate,
    Who has from a mob to choose a mate!
    'Tis a strange and painful mystery!

But the more the eggs, the worse the hatch;
The more the fish, the worse the catch;
The more the sparks, the worse the match;
  Is a fact in woman's history.
Thomas Hood (1799–1845) Miss Kilmansegg,
1869, st. ccvi.

57. At first a woman doesn't want anything but a husband, but just as soon as she gets one, she wants everything else.
Edgar Watson Howe (1853–1937) Country Town
Sayings, 1911.

58. To be today's real woman, you need to have the physique of Venus, the cunning of Cleopatra, the courage of Joan of Arc, the wardrobe of Marie Antoinette, and the cleaning ability of Ammonia D.

    Joyce Jillson *Real Women Don't Pump Gas*, 1982, ch. 4.

59. Sir, a woman's preaching is like a dog's walking on his hind legs. It is not done well; but you are surprised to find it done at all.
Samuel Johnson (1709–1784) Boswell's Life,
31 July 1763.

60. When female minds are embittered . . . their malignity is generally exerted in a rigorous and spiteful superintendence of domestic trifles.
Samuel Johnson (1709–1784) The Rambler, 1751.

61. And a woman is only a woman, but a good cigar is a smoke.
Rudyard Kipling (1865–1936) The Betrothed, 1886.

62. It is because of men that women dislike one another.
Jean de La Bruyère (1645–1696) Characters, 1688,
'Of Women', 55.

63. Women have simple tastes. They can get pleasure out of the conversation of children in arms and men in love.
> H. L. Mencken (1880–1956) *Sententiæ*, in A. Cooke,
> *The Vintage Mencken.*

64. What a woman thinks of women is a test of their nature.
> George Meredith (1828–1909) *Diana of the Crossways*,
> 1885, ch. I.

65. I expect that woman will be the last thing civilized by man.
> George Meredith (1828–1909) *The Ordeal of Richard Feverel*, 1859, ch. I.

66. To be passive in calamity is the province of no woman.
> George Meredith (1828–1909) *ibid.* ch. 35.

67. The subjection of women to men being a universal custom, any departure from it naturally appears unnatural.
> John Stuart Mill (1806–1873) *The Subjection of Women*, 1869 ch. I.

68. What is now called the nature of women is an eminently artificial thing—the result of forced repression in some directions, unnatural stimulation in others.
> John Stuart Mill (1806–1873) *ibid.*

69. Women cannot be expected to devote themselves to the emancipation of women, until men in considerable numbers are prepared to join with them in the undertaking.
> John Stuart Mill (1806–1873) *ibid.* ch. III.

70. Disguise our bondage as we will,
    'Tis woman, woman, rules us still.
> Thomas Moore (1779–1852) *Sovereign Woman.*

71. She affected to establish the character of a woman,
    thoughtless through wit, indiscreet through simplicity,
    but religious on principle.
    > Hannah More (1745–1833) *Cœlebs in Search of a Wife*,
    > 1808, ch. IX.

72. The true value of woman is not diminished by the
    imputation of inferiority in those talents which do not
    belong to her, of those qualities in which her claim to
    excellence does not consist.
    > Hannah More (1745–1833) *Strictures on the Modern
    > System of Female Education*, 1799.

73. Woman was God's *second* mistake.
    > Friedrich Nietzsche (1844–1900) *The
    > Antichrist*, 1888, 48.

74. Woman the fountain of all human frailty!
    What mighty ills have not been done by woman?
    Who was't betrayed the Capitol? A woman.
    Who lost *Mark Anthony* the world? A woman.
    Who was the cause of a long ten years war,
    And laid at last *Old-Troy* in ashes? Woman.
    Destructive, damnable, deceitful woman.
    Women to man first as a blessing giv'n,
    When innocence and love were in their prime,
    Happy a while in Paradise they lay,
    But quickly woman long'd to go astray,
    Some foolish new adventure needs must prove,
    And the first Devil she saw she chang'd her love,
    To his temptations lewdly she inclin'd
    Her soul, and for an apple damn'd mankind.
    > Thomas Otway (1652–1685) *The Orphan*,
    > 1680, act III.

75. People who give their letters large bodies but little else
    live for the present. They enjoy gossip and like being
    socially involved. They are not over interested in
    making money. Women tend to write like this.
    > Jane Paterson, *Know Yourself Through
    > Your Handwriting*.

76. Nothing so true as what you once let fall,
     'Most women have no characters at all.'
>   Alexander Pope (1688–1744) *Epistles to Several Persons*, II, 'To a Lady', l. 1.

77. And yet, believe me, good as well as ill,
     Woman's at best a contradiction still.
>   Alexander Pope (1688–1744) *ibid*. 1.269.

78. To control a woman's nature is to despair of a quiet life.
>   Publilius Syrus (1st Century BC). Quoted in B. House, *From Eve On*.

79. All women are but women.
>   François Rabelais, (*c*. 1494–1553) *Pantagruel*, 1532, book III, ch. XXXII.

80. If women got a slap round the face more often, they'd be a bit more reasonable.
>   Charlotte Rampling, *Observer*, 'Sayings of the Week', 6 March 1983.

81. A woman is like a teabag—only in hot water do you realize how strong she is.
>   Nancy Reagan, *Observer*, 'Sayings of the Week', 3 January 1982.

82. A woman is the most heterogeneous compound of obstinate will and self-sacrifice that I have ever met.
>   Johann Paul Friedrich Richter (1763–1825) *Flower, Fruit and Thorn Pieces*, 1845, book II, ch. V.

83. She had man sense. It was the sixth sense that most women spent all their lives without ever finding.
>   Harold Robbins, *79 Park Avenue*, 1955, book I, ch. 16.

84. Women have been discovered—after a fashion.
>   Barbara Rogers, *The Domestication of Women*, 1980, introduction.

85. Woman was made specially to please man.
> Jean-Jacques Rousseau (1712–1778) *Émile*,
> 1762, book V, part I.

86. Dissimulation is innate in a woman, and almost as much a quality of the stupid as of the clever.
> Arthur Schopenhauer (1788–1860) *Studies in Pessimism*, 1851, 'On Women'.

87. Widow'd wife, and wedded maid,
Betrothed, betrayer, and betray'd.
> Sir Walter Scott (1771–1832) *The Betrothed*, 1825.

88. I thank God I am not a woman, to be touched with so many giddy offences as he hath generally taxed their whole sex withal.
> William Shakespeare (1564–1616) *As You Like It*, 1596–1600, III. ii.

89. Who is't can read a woman?
> William Shakespeare (1564–1616) *Cymbeline*, 1609–10, V. v.

90. Frailty, thy name is woman!
> William Shakespeare (1564–1616) *Hamlet*, 1599–1600, II. ii.

91. She's beautiful, and therefore to be woo'd;
She is a woman, therefore to be won.
> William Shakespeare (1564–1616) *Henry VI*, 1589–90, part I, V. iii.

92. Two women plac'd together makes cold weather.
> William Shakespeare (1564–1616) *Henry VIII*, 1612–13, I. iv.

93. A woman mov'd is like a fountain troubled—
Muddy, ill-seeming, thick, bereft of beauty.
> William Shakespeare (1564–1616) *The Taming of the Shrew*, 1593–4, V. ii.

94. I am asham'd that women are so simple
To offer war where they should kneel for peace,
Or seek for rule, supremacy, and sway,
When they are bound to serve, love and obey.
William Shakespeare (1564–1616) *ibid.*

95. I have no other but a woman's reason;
I think him so, because I think him so.
William Shakespeare (1564–1616) *Two Gentlemen of
Verona*, 1594–95, I. ii.

96. No woman will deny herself the romantic luxury of
self-sacrifice and forgiveness when they take the form
of doing something agreeable.
George Bernard Shaw (1856–1950) *Fanny's First Play*,
1910, act III.

97. Vitality in a woman is a blind fury of creation. She
sacrifices herself to it.
George Bernard Shaw (1856–1950) *Man and
Superman*, 1903, act I.

98. You sometimes have to answer a woman according to
her womanishness, just as you have to answer a fool
according to his folly.
George Bernard Shaw (1856–1950) *An Unsocial
Socialist*, 1884, ch. 18.

99. Women have to unlearn the false good manners of their
slavery before they can acquire the genuine good
manners of their freedom.
George Bernard Shaw (1856–1950) *You Never Can
Tell*, 1898, act IV.

100. The ideal woman is a man, though women lie low and
let that secret keep itself.
George Bernard Shaw (1856–1950) Letter to Ellen
Terry, 21 September 1896.

101. It's a great advantage to women to be regarded as a race apart, an advantage, which, as usual, they abuse unscrupulously.

> George Bernard Shaw (1856–1950). Quoted in Antonia Raeburn, *Militant Suffragettes*, ch. 1.

102. What a nasty mind you have, Bruce. Where did you learn to think like a woman?

> Frank G. Slaughter. *War Surgeon*, 1967.

103. 'Woman and women is two different things', said Suzy. 'Guy knows all about women he don't know nothing about a woman.'

> John Steinbeck (1902–1968) *Sweet Thursday*, 1954, ch. 17.

104. The women were proposed to be taxed according to their beauty and skill in dressing; wherein they had the same privilege with the men, to be determined by their own judgement. But constancy, chastity, good sense and good nature were not rated, because they would not bear the charge of collecting.

> Jonathan Swift (1667–1745) *Gulliver's Travels*, 1726, 'Voyage to Laputa', ch. VI.

105. The woman is the better man.

> Alfred, Lord Tennyson (1809–1892) *The Princess*, 1847, part IV.

106. The woman is so hard
Upon the woman.

> Alfred, Lord Tennyson (1809–1892) *ibid.* part VI.

107. With many women I doubt whether there be any more effectual way of touching their hearts than ill-using them . . . If you wish to get the sweetest fragrance from the herb at your feet, tread on it and bruise it.

> Anthony Trollope (1815–1882) *Miss Mackenzie*, 1865.

108.   She was very much a woman. Self-centred to a degree, the world was made to resolve round whatever concerned her at the time.

Warren Tute, The Rock, 1957, part I, ch. 3, 3.

109.   Women need a lot of attention.

Warren Tute, ibid, part II, ch. 11.

110.   'Tis as hard to persuade a woman to quit anything that makes her ridiculous, as 'tis to prevail with a poet to see a fault in his own play.

Sir John Vanbrugh (1664–1726) The Provok'd Wife,
1698, II. ii.

111.   God created woman only to tame man.

Voltaire (1694–1778). Quoted in B. House,
From Eve On.

112.   The female woman is one of the greatest institooshuns of which this land can boste.

Artemus Ward (1834–1867) Woman's Rights.

113.   Whatever women do they must do twice as well as men to be thought half as good. Luckily, this is not difficult.

Charlotte Whitton (1896–1975). Quoted in M.
Rogers, Contradictory Quotations.

114.   There is only one real tragedy in a woman's life. The fact that her past is always her lover, and her future invariably her husband.

Oscar Wilde (1854–1900) An Ideal Husband,
1899, act III.

115.   We women adore failures. They lean on us.

Oscar Wilde (1854–1900) A Woman of No Importance,
1893, act I.

116.   Twenty years of romance make a woman look like a ruin; but twenty years of marriage make her something like a public building.

Oscar Wilde (1854–1900) ibid.

117. The history of women is the history of the worst form of tyranny the world has ever known. The tyranny of the weak over the strong. It is the only tyranny that lasts.

> Oscar Wilde (1854–1900) *ibid.* act III.

118. Women are a fascinatingly wilful sex. Every woman is a rebel, and usually in wild revolt against herself.

> Oscar Wilde (1854–1900) *ibid.*

119. Women are pictures. Men are problems. If you want to know what a woman really means—which, by the way, is always a dangerous thing to do—look at her, don't listen to her.

> Oscar Wilde (1854–1900) *ibid.*

120. Many ladies are delicately miserable, and imagine that they are lamenting the loss of a lover, when they are full of self-applause, and reflections on their own superior refinement. Painful feelings are prolonged beyond their natural course, to gratify our desire of appearing heroines, and we deceive ourselves as well as others.

> Mary Wollstonecraft (1759–1797) *Thoughts on the Education of Daughters*, 1787, 'Dress'.

121. Would men but generously snap our chains, and be content with rational fellowship instead of slavish obedience, they would find us more observant daughters, more affectionate sisters, more faithful wives, more reasonable mothers—in a word, better citizens.

> Mary Wollstonecraft (1759–1797) *A Vindication of the Rights of Woman*, 1792, ch. IX.

122. A woman of talents, if she be not absolutely ugly, will always obtain great power—raised by the weakness of her sex.

> Mary Wollstonecraft (1759–1797) *ibid.* ch. XII.

123. How can women be just or generous, when they are the slaves of injustice?

> Mary Wollstonecraft (1759–1797)
> *ibid.* ch. XIII, sect. IV.

124. Women have served all these centuries as looking-glasses possessing the magic and delicious power of reflecting the figure of man at twice its natural size.

> Virginia Woolf (1882–1941) *A Room of One's Own*, 1929.

125. As a woman, I have no country. As a woman I want no country. As a woman my country is the whole world.

> Virginia Woolf (1882–1941) *Three Guineas*, 1938, 3.

105. Work

1. Man may work from sun to sun
   But woman's work is never done.

> Anonymous.

2. A woman's work is never done
   As gossiping is far more fun.

> Anonymous.

3. Men are vain, but they won't mind women working so long as they get smaller salaries for the same job.

> Irvin Shrewsbury Cobb (1876–1944). Quoted in N. Bentley and E. Esar, *The Treasury of Humorous Quotations*.

4. The pressure of male trade unions appears to be largely responsible for that crowding of women into comparatively few occupations, which is universally recognised as a main factor in the depression of their wages.

    > F. Y. Edgeworth (1845–1926) 'Equal Pay to Men and Women for Equal Work', *Economic Journal*, December 1922.

5. God only invented dirt and grime to keep women busy.

    > Krystyna Grycuk. Attributed.

6. More women than ever before in our history are relying on themselves instead of Prince Charming. Work is the vehicle that permits this.

    > Elizabeth Nickles and Laura Ashcraft *The Coming Matriarchy*, 1981, ch. 1.

7. Women who work are much more likely to wander than those who don't.

    > Piers Paul Read, *Observer*, 'Sayings of the Week', 24 July 1983.

Index of Authors and Sources

In this index the entries refer to individual quotations rather than pages. Each entry contains two numbers, the first of which indicates the number of the topic and the second the actual quotation. For example, under Addison, the first reference is 4.1. This refers to the 1st quotation appearing under the 4th topic, which is 'Advice'. The numbers and titles of the topics appear at the top of the pages.

Index of Key Words

Like the index of authors and sources, the entries in this index refer not to pages but to individual quotations. Each reference contains two numbers, the first of which indicates the number of the topic and the second that of the actual quotation.

Alimony: wages of sin is a. 32.3
Altar: Aisle, A., Hymn 14.6
In the olden times sacrifices were made at the a. 65.36
Ammonia D: need to have . . . the cleaning ability of A. 104.58
Amusing: she knows the whole art of being a. 91.17
Anatomist: who is an excellent a. 93.1
Ancient: The a. British women 25.1
Angel: good o' calling a young 'ooman a wenus or a a. 43.2
wives who are a.s in the street 103.21
women would rather talk with a man than an a. 104.52
woman yet think him an a. 67.58
Anger: Topic 6
a.'s lost upon you 6.1
Animal: Man . . . what a horrible a. 66.38
woman . . . an a. that delights in finery 104.5
Anthony: Who lost Mark A. the world? 104.74
Anthropologists: worthy of study by the a. . . . marriage 99.1
Antoinette: need to have . . . the wardrobe of Marie A. 104.58
Aphrodisiac: no more powerful a. than success and power 48.19
Appeal: Sex a. is fifty per cent what you've got 85.8
Apple: for an a. damn'd mankind 104.74
since Eve ate a.s 44.1
April: Men are A. when they woo 65.37
Apron: despise one who . . . is always hanging at their a.
strings 67.14
Archaeologist: a. is the best husband 5.9
Argument: Topic 7
Armour: Conceit is the finest a. 21.1
Arrogant: man's a. assumption of superior knowledge 57.2
Art: Topic 8
a. of being a woman 67.27
Artistic: Don't ever wear a. jewellery 59.2
Asleep: hard man . . . you'll mostly find him a. 66.69
Ass: pleased to see a man look like an a. for me 63.34
Asset: virgin . . . a frozen a. 96.3
Athletics: without any reservations about whether . . . a. are
suitable 35.12
Attained: husband is the a. and distained 52.24
Attention: a danger for a husband to pay any a. to his wife 53.18
exchanges the a. of many men for the inattention of one 65.35
so much more a. paid to them while unmarried 48.8
Auntie: A. says, with manner grave 103.23
Aunts: Topic 9
Authority: woman . . . not to usurp a. over the man 104.17

Babes: Bearing b. is a woman's fire and inspiration   17.1
Bachelor: b. is a peacock   66.49
  Home sweet home . . . invented by a b.   51.3
  Never trust . . . a b. too near   66.51
  take a good b. and a good wife   67.52
Bachelors: Topic 10
Bad: Male and female are just as b.   67.30
Baggage: I believe the b. loves me   63.12
Baggages: impossible to live with the b.   104.9
Baking: it's b. powder that keeps him   24.1
Barbed: wears b. wire next to the skin   9.5
Barren: jealous as a b. wife   65.19
Bastards: man imposes no b. on his wife   2.10
Battle: same case with him who runs away from a b.   65.43
Bawd: may she be as ugly as an old b.   65.19
Beach: she's not the only pebble on the b.   27.2
Beast: No wild b. is there   104.8
Beasts: all men are b.   85.7
Beating: What's the good of b. your wife   53.15
Beautiful: All heiresses are b.   98.1
  B. women never have time   58.13
  She's b. and therefore to be woo'd   104.91
Beauty: Topic 11
  No woman can be a b. without a fortune   98.2
  taxed according to their b.   104.104
  we hunt them for the b. of their skins   67.57
Bed: b. with a wife in it   7.5
Behaves: When a woman b. like a man   67.21
Believe: men were born to lie, and women to b. them   67.22
Believes: hard to know what a woman b.   104.3
Bends: Though she b. him, she obeys him   67.28
Betrayer: Betrothed, b., and betray'd   104.87
Bigamy: Topic 12
Bill: A woman that paints puts up a bill   25.4
Bitter: A wife, or b. half   103.4
Blind: happy marriage betwixt a b. wife and a deaf
    husband   65.30
  Men are often b. to the passions of women   63.17
Blondes: b. also prefer gentlemen   11.22
  Gentlemen . . . prefer b.   11.14
Blunders: woman . . . one of nature's agreeable b.   104.34
Blush: Girls . . . bad sign if they don't b.   48.13
  Some women b. when they kiss   60.1
Body: He that possesses a woman's b.   104.7

169

Bondage: Disguise our b. as we will   104.70
Bone: b. when broken, than when made a bride   1.3
    she was really made from his funny b.   1.1
Book: cannot make a good book of cookery   24.2
    women might make excellent b. keepers   15.1
Books: My only b. were woman's looks   27.9
Bore: A healthy male b. consumes each year   91.21
Born: not b., but rather becomes a woman   104.16
Boss: You marry the b.'s daughter   90.4
Bossy: Girls like a man to be a bit on the b. side   48.18
    part of every man . . . resents the great big b. woman   71.10
Bottle: sweetheart is a b. of wine   104.13
Bottles: who eats broken b.   9.5
Bow: As unto the b. the cord is   67.28
Boys: Topic 13
    b. can only help   48.2
    One girl is worth more than twenty b.   48.3
Bracelet: sapphire b. lasts forever   59.3
Brain: b. is not an organ of sex   55.4
Brains: girls prefer beauty to b.   11.1
    What good are b. to a man?   52.39
Bras: Woman's Lib? Put them behind b.   42.3
Brave: takes a b. man to face a b. woman   67.13
Bread: b. and cheese, and kisses   10.14
Break: Husbands . . . require a long time to b. 'em   52.16
Breakfast: must not reheat his sins for b.   46.5
Breeding: hardly distinguish love from good b.   63.42
Bribe: Marriage is a b.   65.51
Bride: bone when broken, than when made a b.   1.3
Brides: Topic 14
Brief: 'Tis b., my lord   63.27
British: The ancient B. women   25.1
Broken: who eats b. bottles   9.5
Brute: Feed the b.   44.2
Brutes: make b.s of [men] and they are . . . faithful   66.70
Build: women should not be expected to . . . b.   67.20
Bus: she would be a b.   9.2
Buses: Men are like b.   66.28
Business: Doing b. without advertising   3.2
    it is a woman's b. to please   104.53
    Men of age . . . seldom drive b. home   5.5
Butterfly: men have no objection to b. minds   55.1

Cages: making nets, and not . . making c.   65.44

170

Calamity: To be passive in c. 104.66
Calmest: c. husbands make the stormiest wives 53.5
Calmness: Nothing is so aggravating as c. 92.3
Camel: husband . . . a mere draught c. for her service 52.36
Capitalist: can't be a feminist and a c. 42.23
Capitol: Who was't betrayed the C.? 104.74
Capture: gins and pitfalls for the c. of men by women 65.38
Careers: Topic 15
Cars: sports c. stick out in front 78.4
Cartesians: furnish a very strong argument to the C. 93.1
Casanova: In this at least every man is . . . a C. 85.9
Cassio: Though C. did some little wrong 6.4
Catch: The more the fish, the worse the c. 104.56
Catches: man . . . chases a woman until she c. him 27.1
Caught: every single girl can be c. 27.10
Certainty: woman's guess is much more accurate than a man's
    c. 57.4
Chained: he is c. to an oar all his life. 52.10
Chains: Would men but generously snap our c. 104.121
Changed: women . . . were never happy until they c. you 49.5
Character: c. he bears among his own sex 104.22
    she affected to establish the c. of a woman 104.71
Characters: Most women have no c. at all 104.76
Charm: as she forgets how to c. 50.7
Charming: Feminine vanity . . . gift which makes women
    charming 95.4
Charms: c. of women were never more powerful 35.5
    woman c. a lover 11.3
Chases: man always c. a woman 27.1
Chastity: Topic 16
    c., good sense and good nature were not rated 104.104
Chatter: able to c. but say nothing 91.7
Chauvinist: even a dedicated feminist needs a c. to lean on 42.7
    I may be a male c. pig, but 42.12
Cheaper: c. plan of marrying again 52.34
Cheer: shall c. up his wife 52.5
Cheerful: wife must be at least as c. as the waitress 51.8
Cheese: bread and c. and kisses 10.14
Chicken: I swear she's no c. 5.18
Child: being able to have a c. is wonderful 48.2
    regard men merely as a means to a c. 42.11
    There is a c. hidden in the true man 66.45
Childish: man is more c. than woman 17.7
Childless: c. men 17.4

Children: Topic 17
　　Men are but c.   66.14
　　weaknesses of the mother will be visited on the c.   71.13
　　wives are like c.   43.3
　　women . . . get pleasure out of the conversation of c.   104.63
Chivalry: Topic 18
Choosing: in c. a wife   103.8
Chores: expected to . . . split half the household c.   66.19
Church: wives who are . . . saints in the c.   103.21
Cigar: good c. is a smoke   104.61
Cinderella: C. married for money   70.1
Cipher: woman . . . reduced to a mere c.   61.8
City: he must be Something in the C.   103.6
Civil: Always be c. to the girls   48.1
　　Women of quality are so c.   63.42
Civility: begets his c. to other people   52.9
Civilized: woman will be the last thing c. by man   104.65
Claret: If I were married to a hogshead of c.   65.46
Clay: Men were made of c.   1.7
Cleaning: need to have the c. ability of Ammonia D.   104.58
Cleopatra: need to have . . . the cunning of C.   104.58
Clever: man likes his wife to be just c. enough   103.25
　　silliest woman can manage a c. man   67.26
Cliches: will now preface his anti-women c.   42.12
Climate: where the c.'s sultry   2.3
Clink: the tinsel c. of compliment   20.1
Clog: The c. of all pleasure   103.19
Clothes: Topic 19
　　bought her wedding c.   4.1
　　Men try to explain the feminine cult of c.   95.1
　　women look at her c.   14.4
Clowns: Men grow such c. when they are married   53.4
Cock: hen should not crow in the presence of the c.   53.12
　　where the hen crows louder than the c.   51.6
Cocks: Why do c. crow early every morning   91.2
Coffee: I'd put poison in your c.   53.1
Cohabitation: usual result of a man's c. with a woman   67.29
Cold: c. as an aunt's kiss   9.1
　　Two women plac'd together makes c. weather   104.92
Colleges: The rule in the women's c.   85.7
Colts: Husbands, like c., are restive   52.16
Command: He loves c. and due restriction   53.9
　　Man to c. and woman to obey   67.56
Commandeth: she c. her husband   73.2

Commanding: courage of a man shown in c. 73.1
Companions: Wives are . . . c. for middle age 103.1
Complain: never any want of women who c. of ill-usage 103.16
Compliments: Topic 20
Composes: Man c., woman interprets 67.8
Conceit: Topic 21
Conquer: Whilst men wish to c. women at large 66.31
Conserves: Man creates, woman c. 67.8
Constancy: Topic 22
  c. . . . were not rated 104.104
Constipated: women are habitually c. 62.4
Consult: Men of age . . . c. too long 5.5
Contempt: c. upon our hobbies of sport, drink and party
    politics 74.3
Content: We are never c. with what we have 49.6
Contraception: Topic 23
Contradict: your words must c. your thoughts 91.5
Contradiction: make us expose ourselves by c. 52.14
  she as well likes c. 53.9
  Woman's at best a c. still 104.77
Conversation: endeavour to give a rational turn to the c. 55.12
  observing his favourite topic of c. 95.2
  Women get pleasure out of the c. of children 104.63
Cooking: Topic 24
  Women just go right on c. 5.17
Coquets: quite as many male c. 27.13
Coquettes: C. are jealous of their lovers 58.6
Cord: As unto the bow the c. is 67.28
Corns: Hell hath no fury like a woman's c. 54.3
Corporation: The c. man 82.1
Corrupt: two sexes mutually c. and improve each other 67.65
Corset: The c. is . . . a mutilation 34.4
Cosmetics: Topic 25
Counsel: hard . . . for women to keep c. 4.3
  woman's c. 1.4
Country: As a woman, I have no c. 104.125
  she may be everything in the c. 103.6
Coupled: C. together for the sake of strife 65.14
Courage: Topic 26
  c. of a man is shown in commanding 73.1
  need to have . . . the c. of Joan of Arc 104.58
Courtship: Topic 27
Cowardice: uses to mask her c. 37.2
Cowards: men of valour, c. to their wives. 26.3

Coy: men should be c., when women woo   27.3
Creates: Man c., woman conserves   67.8
Creation: silliest part of God's c.   63.26
Crouching: c. vassal to the tyrant wife!   104.5
Crow: hen should not c. in the presence of the cock   53.12
   where the hen c.s louder than the cock   51.6
   Why do cocks c. early every morning   91.2
Crowd: every c. of women is a harem broken loose   104.28
Crown: modest silence is a woman's c.   87.6
Cruellest: The c. revenge of a woman   22.1
Crying: Topic 28
   c. over a husband never did any good   52.22
Cuckold: Call your husband a c.   2.1
   What is wit in a wife for, but to make a man a c.   65.53
Cult: try to explain the feminine c. of clothes   95.1
Cunning: need to have . . . the c. of Cleopatra   104.58
   propensity to c. for her own preservation   73.4
Cupid: C. is a knavish cad   63.28
Curiosity: Topic 29

Daddy: D., who 'doesn't understand'   99.1
Daughter: every woman is a man's d.   37.4
   Marry . . . your d. when you can   65.23
   month or two before his d.'s wedding   99.1
   my d.'s my d. all her life   17.5
   only thing a mother don't like her d.   93.11
   remembers not that she was a d.-in-law   72.3
   You marry the boss's d.   90.4
Daughters: Topic 30
   if any of their d. are beauties   71.7
   mothers devour their d.   71.4
Daylight: Lets d. through   102.2
Deadly: female of the species is more d.   40.3
Deaf: marriage betwixt a blind wife and a d. husband   65.30
Deafness: only remedy . . . was the d. of the husband   91.17
Deceit: Topic 31
   men for flattery and d. renowned   43.5
   she knew treachery, rapine, d., and lust   104.36
Deceived: men are always d. on the subject of women   67.3
Deeds: Words are women, d. are men   67.23
Defects: Women love us for our d.   63.40
Defiance: there is no beginning to d. in women   42.18
Deforming: d. their feet   19.4
Deliberates: woman that d. is lost   104.1

Drink: Topic 33
Duel: Marriage is a d. to the death 65.13
Duped: Men are always doomed to be d. 65.24
Duties: another [husband] that performs the d. 52.28
Man can never tell woman that her d. are 66.18
Duty: d. to get married 10.15

Earns: money . . . If she e. it is hers 70.4
Ears: Discreet women have neither eyes nor e. 104.49
Eat: woman that once made him e. up his spinach 71.10
Economics: Topic 34
Education: Topic 35
Eggs: more the e., the worse the hatch 104.56
Elephants: Women and e. never forget an injury 46.7
Elms: Behind the e. last night, cried Dick 96.4
Eloquence: women . . . would carry the e. of the bar to greater
heights 61.1
Emancipate: No fascinating woman ever wants to e. her sex
67.50
Emancipation: history of men's opposition to women's e. 66.74
Women cannot . . . devote themselves to the e. of women
104.69
Embittered: When female minds are e. 104.60
Emigration: when surplus women shall have been removed by
e. 86.5
Emotion: Topic 36
Emotions: in any scheme that involves her e. 36.4
Empire: gained an e. but didn't know how to lose a role
42.13
Engaged: e. man is a lion 66.49
if Adam and Eve had been merely e. 1.8
Engagement: doubt . . . if the same kind of girl is suitable for e. as
for marriage 48.22
England: Lie still and think of E. 14.1
Enterprises: wife and children . . . impediments to great e. 38.2
Envy: conceal their e. of other women 58.6
Equal: e. pay will do something terrible to his gonads 66.43
Women are e. because they are not different 104.43
Equality: Topic 37
only way to insure e. between the two 103.15
very few [examples] of an e. between the sexes 42.10
Erroneous: Men have an extraordinarily e. opinion of their
position 66.37
Errors: share some female e. 11.18

Eve: Adam was first formed then E.   104.17
   Since E. ate apples   44.1
Everest: Housework may not be E.   51.2
Everything: E. they say   66.3
Evils: of two e. choose the prettier   66.67
Exactly: passion for being e. like other men   66.8
Exaggerate: e. the difference between one young woman   48.17
Existence: love . . . 'tis a woman's whole e.   63.7
Experience: triumph of hope over e.   65.25
Extraordinary: it is really e. for a woman   62.6
Extremes: Like other women, I shall run to e.   36.3
Eyes: Discreet women have neither e. nor ears   104.49
   Men are born with two e.   93.4

Face: Every pretty woman studies her f.   95.5
   F. powder may catch a man   24.1
   God has given you one f. and you make yourselves
      another   25.7
   If women got a slap round the f. more often   104.80
   women pardoned all except her f.   46.2
Failure: Women never forgive f.   46.3
Failures: women adore f.   104.115
Fair: never yet a f. woman but she made mouths in a glass   95.11
Faith: Woman's f. is traced in sand   63.5
Faithful: harder to be f. to a mistress   22.4
   men . . . make brutes of them and they . . . are f.   66.70
   to remain f. to a man   22.1
Faithless: F. husbands will make f. wives   53.19
Fall: Women may f., when there's no strength in men   67.48
Falsehood: inconstancy and f. are grounded in their natures
      104.41
Fame: Man dreams of f. while woman wakes to love   67.54
   What's f. with men   67.42
Family: Topic 38
Fancy: In the spring a young man's f. lightly turns   63.33
Farthing: for a f. less   104.2
Fashion: Topic 39
Fat: many jewels make women . . . incredibly f.   59.1
Father: no man is responsible for his f.   71.9
Fathers: F. trust not your daughter's minds   30.3
Faults: All men make f.   66.56
   Every man has his f.   66.48
   Husband without f. is a dangerous observer   52.17
   I can see her f.   104.44

Men's f. do seldom to themselves appear   66.54
To find out a girl's f.   48.5
trivial f. which most offend a husband   52.21
Women have many f.   66.3
Favour: Women introduce into everything f.   67.2
Fawn: men . . . make brutes of them and they f.   66.70
Fear: men keep all women in a state of f.   79.1
Fears: male f. and insecurities   66.57
Feast: Who lets his wife go to every f.   103.9
Feed: F. the brute   44.2
Feels: woman f. more than she thinks   67.8
Feet: deforming their f.   19.4
Female: Topic 40
book of f. logic   7.10
f. woman   104.112
From the tyranny of man . . . f. follies proceed   67.67
no new ideas about f. education   35.3
rarely can a f. mind be impersonal   104.39
When f. minds are embittered   104.60
Feminine: explain the f. cult of clothes   95.1
Feminism is the most unnatural f. activity   42.9
Feminist . . . one who dislikes the chief f. characteristics   42.6
Femininity: Topic 41
Feminism: Topic 42
another name for Sentimental F.   18.1
Fib: Girls . . . bad sign if they don't blush, and f.   48.13
Fickleness: f. of the women I love   22.5
Field: Man for the f. and woman for the hearth   67.56
Fiend: find no f. in hell   6.2
Fierce: more f. and untameable than woman   104.8
Fight: women should not be expected to . . . f.   67.20
Fighters: When women kiss . . . reminds one of prize f.
   60.4
Finery: woman . . . an animal that delights in f.   104.5
Fish: more the f., the worse the catch   104.56
Fishery: ladies of the British f.   61.1
Fishing: if you want to be happy for life go f.   65.5
Fits: She'll have her will, or have her f.   53.9
Flames: Women, like f., have a destroying power   104.30
Flattery: Topic 43
scarce any f. is too gross   11.5
Flesh: marriage makes man and wife one f.   65.15
Flirtation: merely innocent f.   2.4
Flower: worthless f. of beauty   11.19

Habits: bad h. which females acquire 67.66
Had: Every man is to be h. one way or another 67.16
Hair: feminine custom of wearing the h. extremely long 19.5
  Like a woman's h. 11.3
  Sweet girl-graduates in their golden h. 48.20
Half: wife, or bitter h. 103.4
Hand: Give a man a free h. 66.68
Happiness: Topic 49
  fine prospect of h. behind her 14.3
Happy: constant woman . . . but one chance to be h. 22.2
  If you want to be h. for a day, get drunk 65.5
  men can be h. with any woman 63.39
  not a view compatible with a h. marriage 42.21
Harem: every crowd of women is only a h. broken loose 104.28
Hassle: man's home is his h. 51.1
Haste: Married in h., we may repent at leisure 65.18
Hatch: more the eggs, the worse the h. 104.56
Hate: Topic 50
  has beauty enough to make any woman alive h. her 11.9
  men know what they h. 36.2
Hatred: love to h. turn'd 6.3
  no h. so intense and immovable 47.3
He: h. must be Something in the City 103.6
Head: adorn that part of the h. 104.5
  Man with the h. and woman with the heart 67.56
  not so variable a thing in nature as a lady's h. dress 39.1
  support . . . h.s of adult males 104.19
  Woman! What a whirlwind is her h. 104.24
Headache: sick h. is an affectation offering infinite
    resources 54.1
Heart: complains that a young lady has no h. 27.11
  last thing that moves is his h. 93.3
  Man with the head and woman with the h. 67.56
  Once a woman has given you her h. 63.35
  sphere of woman's glories is the h. 67.35
  way to a man's h. is through his stomach 44.3
  With women the h. argues 7.2
Hearth: Man for the field and woman for the h. 67.56
Heaven: H. has no rage 6.3
  women, worst and best, as H. and Hell 67.55
Heiresses: All h. are beautiful 98.1
Hell: find no fiend in h. 6.2
  H. a fury 6.3
  h. for the soul 11.4

H. hath no fury like a woman's corns   54.3
women, worst and best as Heaven and H.   67.55
Helpmate: H. . . . A wife, or bitter half   103.4
Hen: have they not h.-pecked you all?   52.6
   h. should not crow in the presence of the cock   53.12
   where the h. crows louder than the cock   51.6
Hens: while the h. are still asleep   91.2
Herd: women . . . horrible in a h.   104.29
Heroines: desire of appearing h.   104.120
History: happiest women have no h.   49.3
   h. of men's opposition to women's emancipation   66.74
   h. of women is the h. of tyranny   104.117
   Is a fact in woman's h.   104.56
Hit: ere you know you're h.   101.2
Hobbies: h. of sport, drink and party politics   74.3
Hogs: What h. men turn, Belinda   66.65
Hogshead: If I were married to a h. of claret   65.46
Home: Topic 51
   wives who are . . . devils at h.   103.21
Honest: A woman, and ignorant, may be h.   104.33
Honour: woman who has lost her h.   16.5
Hoof: out pops the cloven h.   9.6
Hope: triumph of h. over experience   65.25
Hormones: nothing like gold to get a girl's h. revving up   48.19
Horse: when he abuses his h. or his wife   52.8
   Who lets . . . his h. drink at every water   103.9
   without any reservations about h. riding   35.12
Hosier: been with a man into a h.'s shop   95.1
Hostages: wife and children . . . h. to fortune   38.2
House: man is *so* in the way in the h.   51.4
Household: expected to . . . split half the h. chores   66.19
Housekeeper: bribe to make a h. think she's a householder   65.51
Housework: H. may not be Everest   51.2
Hungry: Man—the h. sinner   44.1
Hunt: enjoys the h. but not the kill   10.2
Hunter: Man is the h.; woman is his game   67.57
Hunting: evolution of a man as a h. carnivore   66.43
Husband: archaeologist is the best h.   5.9
   call your h. a cuckold in jest   2.1
   good wife maketh a good h.   103.10
   got to put up with the life her h. makes for her   103.7
   her future invariably her h.   104.114
   If the h. be not at home   51.5
   if when a h. be obtained she have arrived at her goal   35.18

makes a jealous h. 10.8
marriage betwixt a blind wife and a deaf h. 65.30
marriages are ruined . . . by the common sense of the h. 65.49
never have an educated man for my h. 35.10
Never trust a h. too far 66.51
one h. too many 12.1
only one h. at a time 12.2
only remedy . . . was the deafness of the h. 91.17
She commandeth her h. 73.2
Sometimes a h. enjoys having a jealous wife 58.7
terrifies a h. 11.3
wife is not to be her h.'s judge 103.11
wife . . . pleases her h. 103.18
woman doesn't want anything but a h. 104.57
Husbands: Topic 52
H. cannot be principals 2.5
h. who are least inclined to be tyrants 103.17
London is full of women who trust their h. 94.5
vexed to see h. hate their wives 50.6
women who complain of ill-usage by their h. 103.16
Husbands and Wives: Topic 53
Hymn: Aisle, Altar, H. 14.6
Hypocrite: man who moralises is usually a h. 67.60

Ideal: To nurse a blind i. like a girl 48.21
Ideals: Woman's moral i. are personal and domestic 74.7
Ideas: no new i. about female education 35.3
Ignorant: A woman, and i., may be honest 104.33
Ill: I.-natured as an old maid 65.19
    little judicious i. treatment 103.22
    women who complain of i.-usage by their husbands
    103.16
Illness: Topic 54
Imagination: Does the i. dwell the most 27.14
    lady's i. is very rapid 65.9
Impersonal: rarely can a female mind be i. 104.39
Impossible: i. to live with the baggages 104.9
Improve: two sexes mutually corrupt and i. each other 67.65
Inattention: exchanges the attention of many men for the i. of
    one 65.35
Income: woman's i. chargeable to i. tax 61.2
Inconstancy: i and falsehood are grounded in their natures
    104.41
Indifference: can never look with i. at a woman 66.12

Indiscreet: character of a woman . . . i. through simplicity
   104.71
Indiscretion: I. . . . the guilt of women   104.18
Indiscretions: Women in love forgive large i.   63.22
Ineptitude: He hated her for his i.   50.5
Inequality: There is i. in the sexes   55.5
Inexpensiveness: i. of his wife's clothes   19.1
Inferior: cannot be demonstrated that woman is essentially i.
   37.7
   value of woman is not diminished by the imputation of i.
   104.72
   wife should be i. to the husband   103.15
Infidelities: Women forgive large indiscretions more easily than
   small i.   63.22
Infidelity: offence of i.   2.10
Injury: Women and elephants never forget an i.   46.7
Injustice: women . . . slaves of i.   104.123
Innocence: sort of man who admires i.   67.62
Innocent: merely i. flirtation   2.4
   Very i. girls are usually very stupid   48.10
Inquisitors: good to make severe i.   10.6
Insecure: nothing so i. as an aggressive human male   66.64
Insecurities: male fears and i.   66.57
Inspiration: Bearing babes is a woman's fire and i.   17.1
Institooshuns: female woman is one of the greatest i.   104.112
Intellects: Women . . . will forgive us . . . even our i.   63.40
Intellectual: high degree of i. refinement in the female   35.4
   myth that migraine sufferers are . . . among the i. elite   54.4
   ye lords of ladies i.   52.6
Intelligence: Topic 55
Intelligent: harder to prove you're i.   11.15
   rare as really i. ones   11.20
   woman who thinks she is i.   37.3
Interprets: man composes, woman i.   67.8
Intimacy: To vigorous men i. is a matter of shame   66.44
Intimate: man as i. with his own wife   52.33
Intimidation: Rape . . . a conscious process of i.   79.1
Intoxicated: terrible to see a girl i.   33.2
Intoxication: best of life is but i.   33.1
Intrigue: Topic 56
Intruders: i. in the rights of men   62.3
Intuition: Topic 57
Invention: Woman's virtue is man's greatest i.   97.4
Iron: men, contrary to i.   66.23

if she say yes she's no l. 85.1
Jack is the l. not Jill 103.14
Language: men and women do not speak the same l. 67.3
Lap: L. . . . One of the most important organs of the female 104.19
Lapel: don't want to be the rose on my husband's l. 65.45
she plucked from my l. 104.48
Laugh: Women l. when they can 104.50
Laughing: one thing that stops women l. at them 66.22
Law: Topic 61
secret rebellion against the existing l. 17.9
should be a l. passed 10.16
Lazy: There are no ugly women, only l. ones 25.6
Learn: Let the women learn in silence 104.17
Learning: opinions upon . . . l. 5.19
Lecture: dreads a curtain l. worse than hell 103.5
Legend: l. of the jungle heritage 66.43
Leisure: Married in haste, we may repent in l. 65.18
Letters: dangerous if you keep love l. 63.14
No respectable girl ever reads love l. 48.14
Lewd: A l. bachelor 10.8
Lib: What women's l. does to a woman 42.21
Liberation: sad day for sexual l. 76.2
Since l. the jokes have gained a new element 42.12
Liberty: females will forgive a l. 46.4
Lie: L. still and think of England 14.1
men were born to l., and women to believe them 67.22
nothing about which men l. so much as 85.9
Life: latter part of a wise man's l. 66.63
Lint: invisible strand of l. 104.48
Lion: engaged man is a l. 66.49
Literature: Topic 62
turn her into l. 104.37
Live: Every man desires to l. long 5.21
Lived: would be a thousand pities if women . . . l. like men 67.69
Livelihood: Marriage is for women the commonest mode of l. 85.12
Living: girls . . . how they must hate to work for a l. 48.15
Lock: wife keeps her man under close l. and key 103.14
Logic: book of female l. 7.10
Lollipops: sugar plums and l. of love 103.22
London: L. is full of women who trust their husbands 94.5
Looking-glass: L. to her is what a book is to a pedant 95.5

Looking-glasses: Women have served as l.   104.124
Looks: My only books were woman's l.   27.9
Lord: Thy husband is thy l.   53.14
Lost: Upon a woman won or l?   27.14
Love: Topic 63
   administer small quantities of l. and kindness   103.22
   art of gaining the l. of his wife   103.13
   In revenge and in l. woman is more barbarous   81.4
   lady's imagination . . . jumps from admiration to l.   65.9
   l. match was the only thing for happiness   49.2
   l. to hatred turn'd   6.3
   man can deceive a woman by pretending l.   31.3
   man . . . cannot l. a woman so well   90.3
   Man dreams of fame while woman wakes to l.   67.54
   No respectable girl ever reads l. letters   48.14
   opinions upon l.   5.19
   practice l. in the afternoon   85.7
   sugar plums and lollipops of l.   103.22
   virgin's bloodless l.   96.6
   woman who marries to l. better   65.54
   women . . . bound to serve, l., and obey   104.94
Loved: woman once l. is the most hateful   50.1
Lover: lamenting the loss of a l.   104.120
   her past is always her l.   104.114
   husband is what is left of the l.   52.30
   woman charms a l.   11.3
Lovers: Topic 64
   Coquettes are jealous of their l.   58.6
Luck: Women try their l.; men risk theirs   65.48
Luggage: the l. of life   103.19
Lust: She knew treachery, rapine, deceit and l.   104.36
Lustful: when men are in a l. mood   85.4

Macho: M. does not prove mucho   66.24
Mad: All jealous women are m.   58.10
   Stupidity often saves a man from going m.   55.6
Mafia: One joins a kind of women's m.   71.8
Maid: Ill-natured as an old m.   65.19
Maids: m. are May when they are m.   65.37
   Old m. never like . . . their sisters-in-law   88.1
   Three little m. from school are we   48.6
Male: Advertising: agent of m. supremacy   3.3
   female of the species is more deadly than the m.   40.3

Negative: man . . . becomes a n. thing 38.4
Neglected: a cooling but pretty constant n. 103.22
Neglected: n. wife is . . . the best mother 71.12
Nerve: what is left of the lover after the n. has been
    extracted 52.30
Nervous: Men are n. of remarkable women 66.7
Nets: young ladies spend their time in making n. 65.44
News: He that tells his wife n. 52.18
Newspaper: Reading someone else's n. 2.2
Nice: n. man is a man of nasty ideas 66.62
Night: a beauty at n. 11.17
No: If a lady says n. 85.1
    Since maids, in modesty, say N. 48.16
Nude: The female n. 8.3
Nurses: Wives are . . . old men's n. 103.1

Oak: Man's the o., woman's the ivy 67.9
Oar: he is chained to an o. all his life 52.10
Obedience: Topic 73
Obey: Man to command and woman to o. 67.56
    women . . . bound to serve, love and o. 104.94
Obeys: Though she bends him, she o. him 67.28
Object: Men of age o. too much 5.5
    takes two to make a woman into a sex o. 85.11
    woman who longs to be a sex o. 42.16
    Women have . . . one o. 11.5
Objects: when you stop treating them as sex o. 85.15
Obliged: should be o. to marry a woman 65.40
Obscene: Women should be o. 87.4
Obstinate: woman is the most heterogeneous compound of o.
    will 104.82
Odd: every man is o. 66.55
Offences: woman, to be touched with so many giddy o. 104.88
Opinion: man . . . the o. he has of himself 83.2
    Men have an extraordinarily erroneous o. of their position
    66.37
    men . . . mean o. they have of themselves 43.7
    wonderful how far a fond o. of herself 95.12
Opinions: infer what a man's wife is like, from his o. about
    women 52.25
Orang-utang: husbands remind me of an o. 52.3
Ornaments: all sorts of o. 11.7
Orphan: teach the o. boy to read . . . the o. girl to sew 35.16
Ownership: act of a woman to proclaim o. 104.48

Rake: every woman is at heart a r.   67.41
   man's a r.   66.26
Rape: Topic 79
Rapine: She knew treachery, r., deceit and lust   104.36
Rapist: Men are stereotyped into the types of suppressed r.   42.5
Rational: each sex will wish to appear more or less r.   67.36
Read: teach the orphan boy to r.   35.16
   Who is't can r. a woman?   104.89
Reading: difficult to keep their wives from r.   103.2
Real: feminists do not like r. women   42.1
   how do you remain a r. man?   66.19
Reason: I have no other but a woman's r.   104.95
   Women never r.   104.46
Reasoning: type of mind which is not adept at r.   57.1
Rebel: Every woman is a r.   104.118
Rebellion: than ever lost it [command] by their wives' r.   52.13
Reheat: must not r. his sins for breakfast   46.5
Religion: Topic 80
   opinions upon . . . r.   5.19
Religious: character of a woman . . . r. on principle   104.71
Remarkable: Men are nervous of r. women   66.7
Repent: Married in haste, we may r. at leisure   65.18
   Men of age . . . r. too soon   5.5
Reproductive: If most women . . . see themselves chiefly as r.
   females   42.22
Reputation: fame . . . is call'd in women only r.   67.42
Resemble: The more their sex tries to r. ours   42.17
Retire: men reach their sixties and r.   5.17
Revenge: Topic 81
   cruellest r. of a woman   22.1
   Woman would scarcely take a more complete r.   42.11
Rib: not true that woman was made from man's r.   1.1
Ribald: Man's a r.   66.26
Ribs: wish Adam had died with all his r.   1.2
Rich: No r. man is ugly   98.4
   why I won't marry a r. wife   103.15
Ridicule: R. has pursued the feminist down the corridors of
   time   42.8
Right: divine r. of husbands   52.40
Rights: intruders in the r. of men   62.3
   Let woman share the r.   97.7
Rings: r. put through the nose of the gentleman   99.3
Rival: woman has no greater r.   8.1
Rivals: women are all r.   47.4

Serious: Men love war because it allows them to look s.   66.22
Serpent: talked with the s.   1.8
Servant: men regarded women as a s. class   42.14
Serve: women . . . bound to s., love and obey   104.94
Servitude: bow your neck to the yoke in voluntary s.   22.3
Sew: teach the orphan girl to s.   35.16
Sex: Topic 85
   In certain men, digestion and s. absorb the vital force   66.17
   raised by the weakness of her s.   104.122
   The less there is of s. about a woman   104.54
   While man *has* a s., woman *is* a s.   67.10
   woman never forgets her s.   104.52
   woman who longs to be a s. object   42.16
Sexism: Topic 86
Sexual: sad day for s. liberation   76.2
Shallow: Woman is not even s.   67.40
Shameless: worse than a s. woman   104.10
She: that s. may be everything in the country   103.6
Shock: front-line masculine s. troops   79.2
Shoes: If you would make a good pair of s.   93.10
Shows: He that s. his wife or money   103.24
Silence: Topic 87
   Let the women learn in s.   104.17
Silliest: s. woman can manage a clever man   67.26
Simplicity: character of a woman . . . indiscreet through
      s.   104.71
Sin: wages of s. is alimony   32.3
Single: While you're s.   10.3
Sinner: Man—the hungry s.   44.1
Sins: Men . . . commit more bold, impudent s.   26.4
Sisters: Topic 88
Sixpence: has not s. but in her possession   103.5
Skirt: tenacious attachment to the s.   19.5
Skullion: S. had little use for contraceptives   23.2
Sky: s. changes when they are wives   65.37
Slack: In marriage, a man becomes s.   66.60
Slap: If women got a s. round the face   104.80
Slave: Can man be free if woman be a s.   67.51
   no more like another man than a galley s.   52.10
   not a forced s. but a willing one   66.41
   Wife is synonym for s.   103.23
Slavery: s. of women means the tyranny of women   67.50
   Women . . . false good manners of their s.   104.99
Slaves: men are the s. of fashion   39.2

number of women are not s. in the marriage state   65.52
women . . . s. of injustice   104.123
Sleep: I say I don't s. with married men   2.7
   Never s. with a woman   4.2
Sleeping: like s. with someone else's wife   2.2
Sleeps: When a man s.   66.29
Slight: females will forgive a liberty, rather than a s.   46.4
Slighted: woman!—scorned! s.!   6.2
Sly: Men will have it we are tricky and s.   66.4
Smiles: does not disagree, but s.   7.9
Smoke: good cigar is a s.   104.61
Snares: world is strewn with s., traps . . . for the capture of
   men   65.38
Social Class: Topic 89
Son: every man is a woman's s.   37.4
   Marry your s. when you will   65.23
   my s.'s my s. till he gets a wife   17.5
Sons: Men compete with their s.   71.4
Soup: A wife is only a man's s.   52.27
Sovereign: Thy husband is . . . thy s.   53.14
Sparks: The more the s., the worse the match   104.56
Speaking: S. to . . . a husband never did any good   52.22
Species: female of the s. is more deadly   40.3
Spiteful: rigorous and s. superintendence of domestic trifles
   104.60
Spleen: The s. . . . is a female frailty   92.1
Sport: Men are the s. of circumstance   66.11
Spouse: Prefer a s. whose age is short of thirty   5.6
Spring: In the s. a young man's fancy lighty turns   63.33
Status: in advance of the female in economic s.   34.2
   What a man 'does' defines his s.   67.43
Stomach: way to a man's heart is through his s.   44.3
Stomachs: [men] . . . are all but s.   67.46
Stormiest: calmest husbands make the s. wives   53.5
Stormy: I've seen your s. seas and s. women   64.1
Stoutest: Women . . . make the s. men turn tail   104.23
Strife: Coupled together for the sake of s.   65.14
Strong: woman . . . how s. she is   104.81
Study: noblest s. for womankind   35.2
Stupid: all you have to do is stand still and look s.   48.9
   just s. enough to admire it   103.25
Stupidity: Masculinity and s. are often indistinguishable   66.40
   s. often saves a man from going mad   55.6
Subjection: dogma of women's complete historical s.   104.14

man who t. backwards   55.2
What a woman t. of women   104.64
Thought: Wherever one looked, men t. about women   67.68
Thoughtless: character of a woman, t. through wit   104.71
Three: only t. things to be done with a woman   104.37
Tinsel: the t. clink of compliment   20.1
Tongue: Topic 93
  begins wi' the t.   7.4
  That man that hath a t., I say, is no man   43.6
Tooth: Poison more deadly than a mad dog's t.   58.12
Toys: the price of their t.   13.2
Tractable: men . . . are far more t. in cold blood   66.23
Trade unions: pressure of male t.   105.4
Tragedy: only one real t. in a woman's life   104.114
Traitor: false old t.   5.1
Traps: world is strewn with . . . t. . . . for the capture of
  men   65.38
Treachery: She knew t., rapine, deceit, and lust   104.36
Treason: murder of a man by his wife was called t.   61.6
Treasure: He that weds for t.   11.10
Treasures: virtuous women are hidden t.   97.3
Treatment: a little judicious ill t   103.22
Tree: no man manages his affairs as well as a t. does   66.58
Tricks: Women are like t.   104.31
Tricky: Men will have it we are t. and sly   66.4
Trifles: She who t. with all   27.6
Trigamy: punishment called t.   12.3
Triumph: t. of hope over experience   65.25
Trivial: t. faults which most offend a husband   52.21
Troops: front-line masculine shock t.   79.2
Troubles: woman whose t.   4.2
Troy: And laid at last old T. in ashes   104.74
True: No man worth having is t. to his wife   52.35
  she may be t. to you   94.1
Trust: Topic 94
  Never t. a husband too far   66.51
  never t. a woman   5.23
  T. no man   66.32
  T. not a man with a too caressing tongue   93.2
  T. not a woman when she cries   28.2
Tug: forced to t. a leaky vessel into the bargain   52.10
Turkey: as if someone were to force me to eat t. only   63.24
Twice: women must do t. as well as men   104.113
Tyranny: From the t. of man . . . female follies proceed   67.67

Virtues: Men's . . . v. we write in water   66.53
Vitality: V. in a woman is a blind fury of creation   104.97
Vote: Give women the v.   10.12
Vows: Let no woman believe a man's v.   85.4
   Men's v. are women's traitors   66.52

Wages: w. of sin is alimony   32.3
   women . . . depression of their w.   105.4
Waitress: wife must be at least as cheerful as the w.   51.8
Wander: women . . . more likely to w.   105.7
Wanton: W. as a young widow   65.19
War: Man shall be trained for w.   67.39
   Men love w. because it allows them to look serious   66.22
   Who was the cause of a long ten years w.   104.75
Wardrobe: need to have . . . the w. of Marie Antoinette   104.58
Wash: Men . . . natural disposition to weep and w. up   42.5
   woman that once made him . . . w. behind his ears   71.10
Water: girl promises her lover ought to be written on w.   64.2
   Woman's love is writ in w.   63.5
   Women's weapons, w. drops   28.4
Way: Man has his will . . . woman has her w.   67.24
   woman will have both her word and her w.   93.6
Weak: It is the w. petty mind   81.3
Weakness: raised by the w. of her sex   104.122
   w. of the mother will be visited on the children   71.13
Wealth: Topic 98
Weapon: tongue is a woman's w.   93.7
Weapons: Women's w., water drops   28.4
Weather: Two women plac'd together makes cold w.   104.92
Wedding: all pretty on their w. day   14.2
   before she has bought her w. clothes   4.1
   you may get the w. dresses ready   91.4
Weddings: Topic 99
Weeds: buy yourself w. and be cheerful   101.7
Weep: man may w. on his wedding day   99.2
   Men . . . natural disposition to w. and wash up   42.5
   Women . . . w. when they will   104.50
Wencher: as much mistaken as the w. who marries   65.54
Wheedling: By her we first were taught the w. arts   84.2
   Let no woman believe a man's w. talk   85.4
Wheels: If my aunt had w.   9.2
Whip: A quarrel may end wi' the w.   7.4
Whirlwind: Woman! What a w. is her head   104.24
Wicked: woman may be as w. as she likes   11.16

Widow: Wanton as a young w.   65.19
Widowers: Topic 100
Widows: Topic 101
Wife: bed with a w. in it   7.5
   jealous as a barren w.   65.19
   law . . . refuses to admit the evidence of a w.   61.3
   like sleeping with someone else's w.   2.2
   man imposes no bastards upon his w.   2.10
   marriage betwixt a blind w. and a deaf husband   65.30
   my son's my son till he gets a w.   17.5
   neglected w. is the best mother   71.12
   Next to no w., a good w. is best   65.22
   No man should have a secret from his own w.   83.8
   old bachelor marries a young w.   10.13
   One w. is too much   12.4
   only guy that shouldn't . . . pick . . . out a w.   65.41
   only hope that keeps up a w.'s spirits   101.6
   owes his success to his first w.   90.2
   poor man's w. is the happiest   49.7
   remedy against this interminable talking of the w.   91.17
   she has no vice that I know of, but she's a w.   65.45
   Sometimes a husband enjoys having a jealous w.   58.7
   take a good bachelor and a good w.   67.52
   What is wit in a w. for, but to make a man a cuckold?   65.53
   When a man hath taken a new w.   52.5
   w. is a wine bottle   104.13
   w. must be at least as cheerful as the waitress   51.8
Wilful: Women are a fascinatingly w. sex   104.118
Will: happiness of a man is, 'I w.'   49.4
   Man has his w. . . . woman has her way   67.24
   she'll have her w., or have her fits   53.9
   woman . . . most heterogeneous compound of obstinate
      w.   104.82
Wine: Gentlemen do not throw w. at ladies   66.66
   sweetheart is a bottle of w.   104.13
Winking: like w. at a girl in the dark   3.2
Wire: wears barbed w. next to the skin   9.5
Wisdom: there's w. in women   104.21
Wise: latter part of a w. man's life   66.63
Wit: Topic 102
   What is w. in a wife for, but to make a man a cuckold?   65.53
Witch: try marrying a w.   65.8
Without: four virgins wait w.   96.1
Wives: Topic 103

Fond w. do by their husbands   44.4
men of valour, cowards to their w.   26.3
sky changes when they are w.   65.37
w. are like children   43.3
Woman: any w. alive hate her   11.9
cruellest revenge of a w.   22.1
Every w. knows that   103.3
every w. should marry and no man   65.20
fury of a disappointed w.   6.2
he who is man enough will release the w. in w.   66.46
Home is the . . . w. 's workhouse   51.9
If one w.'s virtue depended on another's suspicions   97.2
like a w. scorn'd   6.3
Man can never tell w. what her duties are   66.18
Man created w.   1.6
never trust a w.   5.23
No w. can be a beauty without a fortune   98.2
she finally began to enjoy being a w.   41.2
slow in words is a w.'s only virtue   91.20
sort of w. a man never gets tired of   67.62
tongue is a w.'s weapon   93.7
very little wit is valued in a w.   102.3
What does a w. want?   78.1
w. seldom asks advice   4.1
w.'s work is never done   105.1 and 105.2
w. was made of man   1.7
w. who breaks her marriage vows   2.9
W. would scarcely take a more complete revenge   42.11
Womanishness: answer a woman according to her w.   104.98
Womb: as her w. fills, her head empties   17.1
Women: Topic 104
All w. become like their mothers   71.11
ancient British w.   25.1
feminists do not like real w.   42.1
fickleness of the w. I love   22.5
happiest w. . . . have no history   49.3
Married w. are kept w.   103.20
no ugly w., only lazy ones   25.6
Plain w. know more about men   11.11
slavery of w. means the tyranny of w.   67.50
What difference does it make whether w. rule   74.2
Whatever you say against w.   1.7
With w. the heart argues   7.2
wit . . . most difficult to pardon in the w.   102.1

w. are not as young as they are painted   25.3
w. cease to be altogether necessary   17.6
W. come in two types   3.1
W. have . . . one object   11.5
W. just go right on cooking   5.17
w. might make excellent book-keepers   15.1
W. must have the last word   7.6
W. . . . never disarmed by compliments   20.2
W. represent the triumph of matter over mind   67.63
w. set such store by sentimental things   14.5
W.'s weapons, water drops   28.4
Won: every woman may be w.   26.2
   Upon a woman w. or lost?   27.14
Woo: Men are April when they w.   65.37
Wooing: Men . . . are always w. goddesses   65.24
Word: Women must have the last w.   7.6
Wordless: w. women, which is silent thunder   87.3
Words: W. are women, deeds are men   67.23
Work: Topic 105
   corset . . . rendering her . . . unfit for w.   34.4
   girls . . . how they must hate to w. for a living   48.15
Worker: wife is a productive w.   52.34
Workhouse: Home is the . . . woman's w.   51.9
Works: Nobody w. as hard for his money   27.7
World: It is a man's w.   66.2
   stop Miss W.   11.2
Worship: w. of beauty   11.23
Worst: appeal to what is w. in him   66.70
Write: I know not what you w. to girls   48.12
   Women should not be expected to w.   67.20
   Women tend to w. like this   104.75
Wrong: climbed the ladder of success w. by w.   90.7
Wrote: would be a thousand pities if women w. like men   67.69

Yawn: Married man can be expected to y.   87.1
Yoke: bow your neck to the y.   22.3
Young: old bachelor marries a y. wife   10.13
   women are not as y. as they are painted   25.3
   y. and not so y.   3.1
   Y. men soon give   5.1